Introduction

This exam preparation book is just that, a preparation book. ....u completing the prep exam within the book will not guarantee a 'pass' on the exam. This book will provide you with an understanding of how the exam will be presented with similar focus on questions that may be presented to you on the actual exam.

The questions and scenarios within this book are not and will not be the questions you are asked on your exam.

The questions and scenarios are based on the publicly available information from the most current body of knowledge and blueprints for ease of understanding and to supplement your preparation.

This book is structured to ask the same amount of questions per topic based on the most current published body of knowledge and blueprint. An example would be the Introduction to European Data Protection. Per the most current blueprint and body of knowledge, you may be asked between four to ten questions under this particular topic on your exam. You will find between four to ten questions in this book addressing this particular topic.

This book outlines and walks you through one proven and recommended way of preparing for your exam.

Exam Taking Tips

The primary essence of dissecting any exam question is to understand the question being asked.

What is 'it' that the question is asking you?

You have to understand what the question is asking before you can correctly answer the question.

Review and understand the three domains within the body of knowledge, along with each sub domain.

Knowing the domains and their objectives will assist you in being able to recall the correct answer for the question.

This book will assist you in determining what the question is asking you to answer.

Most questions on the exam have one or multiple terms presented to you. An example of a term may be 'Accountability.' Knowing what that definition is and where in the domain(s) it is

1

relevant, will help you determine the correct answer, if the question is asking you about 'Accountability.'

An example question (bonus question for you, the reader) may be:

Which is an example of direct marketing?

A.   an email sent to an individual about an order she has placed for a book
B.   an email sent to an individual promoting a new book which is on sale
C.   a letter addressed to 'the household' about a charity bookstore
D.   an advertisement on a website promoting a new book which is on sale

The correct answer is B. An email sent to an individual promoting a new book which is on sale is an example of direct marketing. The term 'direct marketing' refers specifically to the communication, by whatever means, of any advertising or marketing material directed to particular individuals. This means that data protection laws apply to the sending of marketing messages only where individuals' personal data is processed in order to communicate the marketing message to them. Marketing that does not entail processing of any personal data and is therefore not directed at individuals (for example, untargeted website banner advertisements), is not subject to data protection compliance. In addition, messages that are purely service-related in nature (messages sent to individuals to inform them, for example, about the status of an order they have placed) do not generally constitute direct marketing. The GDPR does, however, provide the data subject the right to object to processing for the purposes of direct marketing. See GDPR Recitals 47 and 70, GDPR Article 21, and Article 29 Working Party Opinion 5/2004.

These types of questions, with that thought process, are highly likely to be presented to you on your exam.

The exam is multiple choice and has numerous scenario-based questions. You have 2 hours and 30 minutes to complete the 90-question exam.

If possible, read the questions twice to help you truly understand the question being asked.

If you read the question and know the answer before you look below to the presented answers, trust that intuition. Look at the presented answers to confirm the correct answer.

If your answer is not presented in the answers, look for a similar answer. That 'similar' answer may be your correct answer.

If neither of those answers are presented, re-read the question. Look for the key 'term' and see if there is a word, such as 'any' or 'all' or if the question is asking you for 'what is NOT' a part of the term or question. Those keywords will help you identify possible distracting, presented answers and lead you to eliminate those from the equation of possible questions.

You will then have two good or best answers to select from once you have completed that process.

Reflect on the definitions and terms that you have studied along with your experience to decipher the correct response. Mark that question and move on to the next question.

Learn the terms and definitions, please!

The terms and definitions make up a large portion of the overall content. Utilize those in your day-to-day responsibilities from the point you start preparing for your exam. That will reinforce the terms, their definitions and potentially also prepare you for your future exams.

FINAL PREP

The first time you read the exam question is to train your mind to quickly reflect on the key words you read and what is being asked.

Reading a question twice will highlight those key-words and begin to clarify what the question is really asking you to answer.

Reflect on those keywords. Terms. Definitions.

Ask yourself what the question is asking you to know.

The first five questions of this book will start you on that process of asking you to read the question twice.

After that, highlight the keywords of the question.

Finally, ask yourself what the question is asking you to know.

Review the questions and choose the correct answer.

Remember, you can flag a question and come back to review it at the end. Do not get frustrated if you don't know the answer.

Don't spend too much time on one particular question. If you are unsure of the answer, flag it, and move on to the next and review ALL flagged items at the end.

Do NOT leave any questions blank or unanswered.

You can also find in our library the CIPM: FOCUSED PREPARATION; the CIPP/US: FOCUSED PREPARATION; and the HCISPP: FOCUSED PREPARATION prep exam books for your use in future exams.

Take your time, prepare as best you can, reference as many resources that you need to feel comfortable and prepared to take the exam.

Now, let's get started with your CIPP/E: FOCUSED PREPARATION and thank you for purchasing this book!

Let's give it a go.

Question 1.

General Data Protection Law (LGPD) is Brazil's first comprehensive data protection law and is designed to enhance the privacy and protection of personal data of individuals in Brazil. The LGPD heavily resembles the EU General Data Protection Regulation (GDPR).

On September 17, 2020, the Brazilian president approved the bill, resulting in the LGPD taking effect on September 18, 2020.

At the end of October 2020, India announced that they are currently working towards a privacy regulation, similar, yet possibly more stringent than GDPR? What will this new law be named?

General Data Protection Law (LGPD) is Brazil's first comprehensive data protection law and is designed to enhance the privacy and protection of personal data of individuals in Brazil. The LGPD heavily resembles the EU General Data Protection Regulation (GDPR).

On September 17, 2020, the Brazilian president approved the bill, resulting in the LGPD taking effect on September 18, 2020.

At the end of October 2020, India announced that they are currently working towards a privacy regulation, similar, yet possibly more stringent than GDPR? What will this new law be named?

Key words: India; privacy regulation

Questions to ask yourself – What is a privacy regulation?

Answers:
A. General Data Protection Regulation (GDPR)
B. Personal Data Protection Act (PDPA)
C. Privacy Data Protection Act (PrDPA)
D. Personal Privacy Rights Act (PPRA)

Question 2.

As the privacy professional of an investment organization, you are providing guidance and review of processes for collecting and processing of personal data collected from your employees.
GDPR Article 88 specifies there are more legislative layers applied and that can be imposed by Member States on what can be collected, when it can be collected and how it is collected and processed. All of the answers below are possible bases for processing personal information. Which one is not a preferred method?

As the privacy professional of an investment organization, you are providing guidance and review of processes for collecting and processing of personal data collected from your employees.
GDPR Article 88 specifies there are more legislative layers applied and that can be imposed by Member States on what can be collected, when it can be collected and how it is collected and processed. All of the answers below are possible bases for processing personal information. Which one is not a preferred method?

Key words: processes; collecting; processing; personal data; employees; not; preferred.

Questions to ask yourself – What is the question asking me or not asking me for?

Which one of the answers below is not preferred for processing data OF employees?

Answers:

A. Consent
B. Contract
C. Legitimate Interest
D. Legal Obligations

Question 3.

Privacy professionals are charged with the protection and appropriate use of?

Privacy professionals <u>are charged</u> with the <u>protection</u> and <u>appropriate use</u> of?

Key words: are charged; protection; appropriate use

Questions to ask yourself – What or why are Privacy Professionals at your organization? What are they responsible for? What or where is their focus?

Answers:

A. Private Information
B. Personal Information
C. Public Information
D. Social Information

Question 4.

On July 16, 2020, the European Union Court of Justice (CJEU) invalidated the EU-US Privacy Shield in its decision in Facebook Ireland v. Schrems (Schrems II). The court determined that the Privacy Shield transfer mechanism does not comply with the level of protection required under EU law.
The decision reinforces the European Union's commitment to protecting what?

On July 16, 2020, the <u>European Union Court of Justice (CJEU)</u> <u>invalidated</u> the <u>EU-US Privacy Shield</u> in its decision in Facebook Ireland v. Schrems (Schrems II). The court determined that the Privacy Shield <u>transfer mechanism</u> does <u>not comply</u> with the <u>level of protection</u> required under EU law.
The decision reinforces the European Union's commitment to protecting what?

Key words: European Union Court of Justice; invalidated; EU-US Privacy Shield; transfer mechanism; not comply; level of protection

Questions to ask yourself – What is being transferred? What did the EU-US Privacy Shield provide organizations?

Answers:

A. Regulations
B. Security
C. Privacy
D. Citizens

Question 5.

Technologies that enable and enhance and preserve privacy and security of data throughout its entire lifecycle while protecting information privacy by eliminating or minimizing personal data is called?

Technologies that enable and enhance and preserve privacy and security of data throughout its entire lifecycle while protecting information privacy by eliminating or minimizing personal data is called?

Key words: Technologies; preserve privacy; data; lifecycle; information privacy; eliminating; minimizing personal data

Questions to ask yourself – What technologies preserve privacy/data?; What is information lifecycle (term)? What does minimizing personal data mean?

Answers:

A. Confidentiality
B. Data Protection
C. Information Security
D. Privacy Enhancing Technologies

That concludes the trial of having the question posed to you twice, highlighting the key words and questions to ask yourself.

There may be a few more of these scattered throughout the answers in the rear of the book to keep reminding you to practice this test taking recommendation.

Question 6.

A framework approved by the European Union and US Government for complying with EU data protection regulations when data is transferred between the European Economic Area (EEA) and the United States is called?

Answers:

A. General Data Protection Regulation
B. Privacy Shield
C. Standard Contractual Clause
D. Binding Corporate Rules

Question 7.

This institution consists of 705 members, seven political groups, 27 committees that the members participate in to prepare the work for plenary sessions. This institution is the EU's only directly elected institution. What institution is this?

Answers:

A. Council of Europe
B. European Parliament
C. European Commission
D. European Council

Question 8.

Members of this institution are the heads of state or government of the 27 EU member states and the President of the European Commission. It is not one of the EU's legislating institutions, so it does not negotiate or adopt EU laws.
Instead, it sets the EU's policy agenda, traditionally by adopting 'conclusions' during its meetings which identify issues of concern and actions to take. What institution is this?

Answers:

A. European Council
B. European Parliament
C. European Commission
D. Council of Europe

Question 9.

You are a resident of a multifamily housing complex and have provided personally identifiable information (PII) to the property management member to tour the complex and available units for possible leasing.

Upon returning to the office, you are provided with either a paper application or a web URL and link to complete and submit an electronic application. The questions are the same on both applications. You complete the application and alert the office representative that you have completed your application.

The office representative begins to review the application and receives approval of your application.

To continue the process and to secure the unit, you are asked to provide more PII that includes your banking information that will be automatically debited on the 1st day of each month for your rent and utilities and a link to a complex website where you can share information, request maintenance and other information.

The property management team is GDPR compliant and provides you with your rights as a data subject. Which of the following are not one of those rights?

Answers:

A. Access
B. Rectification
C. Erasure and the right to be forgotten
D. Right to share

Question 10.

You are a Data Protection Officer (DPO) for a multinational manufacturing organization. You have been in your current role for over 90 days. As part of your role, you have established a working relationship with your Data Protection Authority (DPA).
The DPA discusses matters with other DPA's and supports the cooperation between the EU's DPA's.
The EU's DPA's consistently apply data protection rules throughout the EU, which are contributed to by an independent European body that is composed of representatives of the national data protection authorities. The supervisory authorities of the EFTA EEA States are also members with regard to the GDPR related matters and without the right to vote and being elected as chair or deputy chairs. This Body is established by the General Data Protection Regulation (GDPR) and is based in Brussels. What is this body?

Answers:

A. European Council
B. European Data Protection Authority
C. European Data Protection Board
D. European Data Protection Supervisory

Question 11.

Your organization is coordinating a cross-border effort and is working with the Global Privacy Enforcement Network (GPEN) prior to executing the transfer of data. Which one of the following agencies is not a part of the GPEN?

Answers:

A. European Data Protection Supervisor (EDPS)
B. Federal Commissioner for Data Protection and Freedom of Information
C. Information Commissioner's Office (ICO)
D. Office of Civil Rights

Question 12.

You are the privacy officer for a small healthcare organization that is conducting a self-regulatory self-assessment questionnaire (SAQ). Which one of these would this report best support?

Answers:

A. GDPR
B. EU Directive on Electronic Commerce
C. PCI DSS
D. U.S. HIPAA

Question 13.

A Germany based organization receives its first data subject access request (DSAR). You are the privacy professional for the organization and are alerted to the receipt of the request in a timely fashion. What will you, as the privacy professional, reference, that was developed in the establishment of the privacy program, that will assist in determining where the DSAR's information resides?

Answers:

A. Data Classification Policy
B. Privacy Program Scope
C. Regulatory Map
D. Data Inventory

Question 14.

This milestone document in the history of human rights was drafted by representatives with different legal and cultural backgrounds from all regions of the world, the Declaration was proclaimed by the United Nations General Assembly in Paris on 10 December 1948 (General Assembly resolution 217 A) as a common standard of achievements for all peoples and all nations. It sets out, for the first time, fundamental human rights to be universally protected and it has been translated into over 500 languages. What milestone is this?

Answers:

A. The Universal Declaration of Human Rights
B. The Declaration of the Rights of Man and of the Citizen
C. The United States Declaration of Independence
D. The Magna Carta

Question 15.

Effective on May 25, 2018, this regulation is viewed as the toughest privacy and security law in the world. Though it was drafted and passed by the European Union (EU), it imposes obligations onto organizations anywhere, so long as they target or collect data related to people in the EU. This regulation levies harsh fines against those who violate its privacy and security standards, with penalties reaching into the tens of millions of euros, as we have seen from multiple organizations. Which regulation is this?

Answers:

A. General Data Protection Regulation
B. EU Directive on Electronic Commerce
C. EU Directive on Privacy and Electronic Communication
D. EU Data Protection Directive

Question 16.

Given that children merit specific protection, any information and communication, where processing is addressed to a child, should be in such a clear and plain language that the child can easily understand. This represents which principle?

Answers:

A. Privacy Notice
B. Children's Online Privacy Protection Act
C. Purpose Limitation
D. Transparency principle

Question 17.

You are drafting a statement that is a public document which identifies who the data controller is, with contact details for its Data Protection Officer, which is you. It should also explain the purposes for which personal data are collected and used, how the data are used and disclosed, how long it is kept, and the controller's legal basis for processing.
What is this statement named?

Answers:

A. Privacy Statement
B. Privacy Policy
C. Privacy Notice
D. GDPR Notice

Question 18.

What type of data is not considered to be personal data by the GDPR, as detailed in Article 4(1), and its collection and processing is governed by the GDPR. Article 3(2) states that, "This Regulation applies to the processing of personal data of data subjects who are in the Union."

Answers:

A. Geolocation
B. Online identifier
C. Economic
D. Historic

Question 19.

Your organization moved to a work-from-home (WfH) model in March 2020. During that time frame, before your employees began to return-to-work (RtW) your HR and facility directors reviewed guidelines on all monitoring of employees, ensuring that everyone was and would be safe as they returned to their offices and cubicles.
A new monitoring solution to ensure all RtW employees are wearing masks and keeping social distance is to record, without sound, the common areas and workplace areas of the workforce. What type of monitoring is this?

Answers:

A. Surveillance by public authorities
B. Video surveillance
C. Facial recognition
D. Biometrics

Question 20.

Your organization operates a commercial website and online services that collect and maintain covered information from all of its consumers. Your organization is targeting a number of member states and their residents. Which one of these marketing terms defines this action?

Answers:

A. Telemarketing
B. Direct marketing
C. Online behavioral targeting
D. Web cookies

Question 21.

The Council of Europe invited member states to sign this treaty, which is based on human rights declaration and is an international treaty to protect human rights and fundamental freedoms. This treaty applies only to member states. What treaty is this?

Answers:

A. UN Declaration of Human Rights
B. Convention for the Protection of Human Rights and Fundamental Freedoms
C. Universal Human Rights Declaration
D. Organization for Economic Co-Operation and Development

Question 22.

This was the first legally binding international instrument in the field of data protection and was a defining moment in the development of European Data Protection law.

Answers:

A. UN Human Declarations Right
B. Data Protection Directive
C. General Data Protection Regulation
D. Convention 108

Question 23.

A B2B website features their teams' direct email addresses and telephone numbers for inquiries.
In this situation, you would be allowed to use these contact details to contact the person if you were interested in using their services.
Is it still possible to contact the person to sell your services? If so, what contact information would you be able to use under GDPR?

Answers:

A. Business contact data
B. Personal contact data
C. Social networking services
D. Artificial Intelligence

Question 24.

User consent must be obtained from clear and affirmative actions. Access to online content cannot depend on a visitor's agreement to process their personal data. These are two key points of the recently updated guidelines of the European Data Protection Board on the concept of consent. The guidelines provide recommendations on existing consent practices and make it clear that cookie walls are not compliant with the General Data Protection Regulation.

Your organization is using consent mechanisms, which rely on the use of scrolling, swiping through the webpage or any other form of continued browsing.

The EDPB clarifies that scrolling, swiping or continued browsing do not constitute such unambiguous consent.

None of these activities above can be regarded as providing valid consent under the GDPR.

Access to internet services should not be conditional on the acceptance of cookies. The practice called "Cookie walls" blocks content and prevents users from accessing content unless they consent to certain what?

Answers:

A. Consent
B. Cookies
C. Access
D. Direct Marketing

Question 25.

Your organization is migrating their applications and processes to a cloud computing platform. Accessibility, storage and management are key business drivers for this effort.

All of the following are challenges in cloud computing within GDPR except?

Answers:

A. Data retention
B. Data processing outside of the EEA
C. Data ownership
D. Vendor management

Question 26.

Your customer's information and their rights to control what and who collects their information, where their information is shared are privacy rights. Which of the following is not one of the lawful processing criteria?

Answers:

A. Contractual necessity
B. Sensitive vital information
C. Legal obligations
D. Legitimate interest

Question 27.

In 1996, the Department of Health and Human Services within the United States of America, signed into law the Healthcare Insurance Portability and Accountability Act (HIPAA). HIPAA was created to "improve the portability and accountability of health insurance coverage" for employees between jobs.
Within GDPR, Art. 20 empowers the data subject to have the right receive the personal data concerning him or her, which he or she has provided to a controller, in a structured, commonly used and machine-readable format and have the right to transmit those data to another controller without hindrance from the controller to which the personal data have been provided. This right is what?

A. Access
B. Rectification
C. Data portability
D. Automated decision making

Question 28.

Your organization has conducted and inventoried all data flows, classifying the data elements and its flow, both internally and externally. All data within each lifecycle step have had physical, technical and administrative security controls applied to protect the confidentiality, integrity, and availability of that data.
What might be said about your organization's security measures implemented?

Answers:

A. Adequacy decision
B. Appropriate technical and organizational measures
C. Accuracy and storage
D. Storage limitation

Question 29.

Your organization encrypts and redacts the personal and business critical data it controls. Your organization suffers a data breach. After you have contacted your data breach coach and deploy a forensic investigator, it is determined that your encryption key has not been compromised. Based on Art. 33, who must you notify?

Answers:

A. Data Protection Authority
B. Supervisory Authority
C. Data Protection Officer
D. No one

Question 30.

It is vital that employers view data protection as an obligation to safeguard their employee's personal data, which is also required under employment law and collective agreements with trade unions and other bodies.
In certain cases, processing activities that involve employee data also involves interacting with DPAs, where they may not approve processing unless and until who has been involved?

Answers:

A. HR
B. Legal
C. Work Councils
D. Employees

Question 31.

The GDPR demands clarity through a privacy notice. Your privacy notice must be concise, transparent, intelligible and easily accessible; written in clear and plain language, particularly if addressed to a child; and free of charge.
This means a simple link to your crazy-long privacy policy during registration will likely not do the trick.
What is the preferred method of providing your privacy notice to the public?

Answers:

A. Transparent
B. Short
C. Layered
D. Simple

Question 32.

As your organization decides on what data to collect, it must identify valid business purposes, known as a lawful basis, for collecting and using personal data. Art. 5(1) of the GDPR outlines six data protection principles. Which is the first?

Answers:

A. Purpose limitation
B. Data minimization
C. Accuracy
D. Fairness

Question 33.

In which chronological order were the following frameworks adopted?

Answers:

A. Directive on Privacy and Electronic Communications/Data Protection Directive/Directive on Electronic Commerce/GDPR
B. Data Protection Directive/Directive on Privacy and Electronic Communications/Directive on Electronic Commerce/GDPR
C. GDPR/Directive on Privacy and Electronic Communications/Data Protection Directive/Directive on Electronic Commerce
D. Council 108/Data Protection Directive/Directive on Electronic Commerce/Directive on Privacy and Electronic Communications

Question 34.

GDPR non-compliant fines are based on the specific articles of the Regulation that the organization has breached. Infringements of the organization's obligations, including data security breaches, will be subject to the lower level, whereas infringements of an individual's privacy rights will be subject to the higher level. Data controllers and processors face administrative fines of the higher of €10 million or 2% of annual global turnover for infringements of articles:
8 (conditions for children's consent),
11 (processing that doesn't require identification),
25-39 (general obligations of processors and controllers),
42 (certification), and
43 (certification bodies)

The higher of €20 million or 4% of annual global turnover for infringements of articles:
5 (data processing principles),
6 (lawful bases for processing),
7 (conditions for consent),
9 (processing of special categories of data),
12-22 (data subjects' rights), and
44-49 (data transfers to third countries).

In 2019, British Airways was fined what amount for a 2018 data breach over data security failings which enabled unauthorized access to be obtained to personal and payment card information relating to more than 500,000 of its customers.

Answers:

A. €10 million
B. €20 million
C. €183 million
D. €30 million

Question 35.

Under Art. 82, Right to Compensation and Liability, a controller or processor shall be exempt from liability under para. 2 if it proves that it is not in any way responsible for the event giving rise to the what?

Answers:

A. Processing
B. Data Sharing
C. Damages
D. Cross-border transfers

Question 36.

You are the privacy professional for your organization and are looking to apply data protection principles within your organization's processes.
As you review current processes, you determine that data processing is not being processed for the purposes they were collected for. Which principle do you need to implement?

Answers:

A. Purpose Limitation
B. Data Minimization
C. Accuracy
D. Storage Limitation

Question 37.

Your organization relies on B2B sales, which is competitive by nature. Your sales teams cannot escape GDPR and its reach and regulations. You hold a sales team meeting to discuss the following

Do you still rely on purchased leads to fill up your sales pipeline?

Do you automatically add business card contact data to your mailing list?

Do you ask existing customers for referrals and recommendations?

If you answered "yes" to any of the questions above, then GDPR has an impact on you and your organization.

If you continue to solicit prospects to purchase your products or services, this is called?

Answers:

A. Telemarketing
B. Marketing
C. Email marketing
D. Social network marketing

Question 38.

Your organization is a publicly traded investment company and data protection is critical to your operations. The impact of a successful data breach may have consequences that extend beyond your organization and impacts other market participants and retail investors, who may not be well informed of these risks and consequences.

Your organization has decided to repurpose data. You are reviewing the legitimate interest possibility for the repurposing and processing of personal data. You have conducted three tests to ensure your organization can utilize legitimate purposes for that processing. Two of those tests were the Necessity test and the Balancing of Interest test. What is the third test that must be met?

Answers:

A. Storage
B. Limitation
C. Purpose
D. Legitimate test

Question 39.

The Coronavirus has impacted the globe both personally and professionally. Initial reports in March and April 2020 had five new cases a day being reported in areas, which was viewed as high. On November 4, 2020, over 100k cases were reported in one day within the U.S. What type of processing of personal data is this?

Answers:

A. Legitimate Interest
B. Public Interest
C. Consent
D. Contract

Question 40.

This employment practice is an indispensable element of a functioning compliance management system. All companies with more than 50 employees as well as financial service providers and municipalities with more than 10,000 inhabitants will in future be obliged to set up these systems.
What type of system is this?

Answers:

A. Workplace monitoring
B. Storage
C. Retention
D. Whistleblowing system

Question 41.

You are overall responsible for protecting the data of your organization. That includes business, personal, and employee' data. You need to have visibility to; where the data is, where it's going, and who has access. Network level visibility is fundamental to understanding these questions, but in an environment that allows personally owned devices, any visibility is lost the second the device walks out the door and outside your network.

Your organization is attempting to rectify this issue by making use of Enterprise Mobility Management (EMM) tools for application control and some device-level management, but neglect network level control. For a personal device, this makes sense. It's totally understandable that employees would refuse to install a solution that can see even just a scrap of their online activity. Device-level monitoring of an EMM is about as intrusive as most would allow and indicators of risk go overlooked as a result.

Corporate-owned and issued devices, on the other hand, have a greater degree of control and the script is pretty simple to communicate to employees – "we issue you the device, you use it in-line with corporate acceptable use policy and we monitor activity (the same as we would on your desktop) in order to keep our data safe from hackers". It's less simple when the device is owned by the employee. What type of model is this discussing?

Answers:

A. Bring Your Own Device (BYOD)
B. Shadow IT
C. Virtual Private Network (VPN)
D. IT Lifecycle

Question 42.

The Directive on Patients' Rights in Cross-Border Healthcare provides a legal basis for establishing a network on e-health in order to address such practical issues, focusing in particular on cross-border aspects (such as summary records for cross-border care, identification and secure sharing of information), as well as the vital strategic issue of methods for using e-health to enable use of medical information for public health and research – potentially an answer to address the delays that currently plague health data.

The European Commission also finances a wide range of projects developing and piloting e-health technologies and applications, for example in support of the European Innovation Partnership on Active and Healthy Ageing. E-health is presented as a way to address the shortage of health professionals in the European Union, to ensure better care of ageing populations and chronic diseases putting pressure on health budgets, as well as to remedy unequal quality and access to healthcare services in Europe.
Which Article of the GDPR addresses personal health information?

Answers:

A. Art. 4
B. Art. 5
C. Art. 9
D. Art. 11

Question 43.

Your organization is planning on cross-border transfers from the EU to the U.S. You are working on creating internal rules which define international policy within your multinational organization. What codes of conduct are you creating?

Answers:

A. External codes of conduct for cross-border transfers
B. Internal data protection training
C. Standard Contractual Clauses
D. Binding Corporate Rules

Question 44.

On July 16, 2020, the CJEU invalidated the E.U.-U.S. Privacy Shield, one of the methods for transfers of personal data into the U.S. The court found that under U.S. surveillance laws, the U.S. government has access to personal data that does not provide Europeans with privacy protections equivalent to those in the E.U.
Which answer below is most associated with this ruling?

Answers:

A. Schrems
B. Snowden
C. GDPR
D. Privacy Protection

Question 45.

You are the privacy professional within your organization. Your organization processes personal data wholly or partly by automated means and the processing other than by automated means of personal data which do form part of a filing system or are intended to form a filing system applies to which GDPR article?

Answers:

A. Art. 2
B. Art. 3
C. Art. 1
D. Art. 4

Question 46.

Your organization must share personal information to a country outside of the EEA and EU. You individually tailor the contract to your company's needs and obtain the required supervisory authority's authorization. What type of cross-border transfer rule are you using?

Answers:

A. BCR
B. SCC
C. Codes of Conduct
D. Ad hoc contractual clause

Question 47.

You are the privacy professional within your organization. Your organization processes personal data of data subjects who are in the Union by a controller or processor not established in the Union, where the processing activities are related to the offering of goods or services. Which GDPR article applies?

Answers:

A. Art. 2
B. Art. 3
C. Art. 1
D. Art. 4

Question 48.

An individual is applying for a new, open position listed on a job board website, which is your organization's role. Your organization requires that in the processing of personal data appropriate security of personal data is ensured. This should include protection against unauthorized or unlawful processing, destruction and damage. Appropriate technical or organizational measures are to be taken in order to comply with this requirement: such data security measures can include the use of encryption and authentication and authorization mechanisms.

Which of the six data protection principles is this?

Answers:

A. Accountability
B. Integrity and Confidentiality
C. Security Controls
D. Data Minimization

Question 49.

When a data subject makes an online purchase, a controller processes the address of the individual in order to deliver the goods. Which of the six lawful bases for processing is this?

Answers:

A. Consent
B. Legitimate interest
C. Legal obligation
D. Contractual necessity

Question 50.

Your organization completed the data inventory exercise. What term is explicitly highlighted in Article 6(4)(e) as an "appropriate safeguard" that can be used by data controllers "in order to ascertain whether processing for another purpose is compatible with the purpose for which the personal data are initially collected?

Answers:

A. Data minimization
B. Anonymize
C. Pseudonymization
D. Data encryption

Question 51.

Which data protection principle entails that personal data must be kept in a form that makes it possible to identify data subjects for no longer than is necessary for the purposes of the processing. Keeping these data for longer periods is allowed when the processing of the data will aim at achieving purposes in the public interest, scientific or historical research purposes or statistical purposes. Nevertheless, also in these cases rights and freedoms of data subjects must be safeguarded.

Answers:

A. Purpose limitation
B. Storage
C. Integrity and Confidentiality
D. Accuracy

Question 52.

GDPR does not prevent video monitoring even when the employee does not know or consent to being monitored. Labor unions and work councils may negotiate limitations on video recordings of unionized workers. Union members should speak with a union representative if they have concerns about workplace video monitoring.
Your organization requires these in order to monitor its workforce except?

Answers:

A. Vital interest
B. Public interest
C. Legitimate interest
D. Personal interest

Question 53.

Your organization processes and collects over 1,000,000 credit card transactions annually. You have conducted an assessment on your PCI-DSS compliance. The PCI-DSS deals strictly with payment card data and cardholder information, such as credit/debit card numbers, primary account numbers (PAN), and sensitive authentication data (SAD) such as CVVs and magnetic stripe data, from all the major card schemes.

The GDPR has a much wider scope and covers any personally identifiable information (PII). The type of data in scope for GDPR includes PII related to any EU resident, whether it is connected to his or her private, professional or public life. This can include a name, home address, photo, email address, bank details, medical information, posts on social networking websites, or a computer's IP address.
Your organization suffers a breach that violates PCI DSS compliance, which now, also, violates the GDPR.
Which data protection principle applies here?

Answers:

A. Data minimization
B. Integrity and Confidentiality
C. Storage limitation
D. Purpose limitation

Question 54.

Your organization is conducting a thorough review of all data processing activities executed by the organization.

All of the following were inventoried. Which one is not data processing?

Answers:

A. Shredding documents containing personal data
B. Sending promotional emails
C. Video recording
D. Posting information on its social network

Question 55.

You are receiving unsolicited text messages and calls from multiple political parties during the campaign season. You have contacted the organization that continues to contact you and have asked to be removed from their distribution list.
You then follow up that initial request with a request to have all of your personal data erased. This right to erasure is also known as the right to be forgotten. How long does the organization have to respond to the request?

Answers:

A. 30 days
B. Without undue delay
C. 60 days
D. 31 days

Question 56.

You are making a purchase on an e-commerce website and you receive a notice in the middle of the page that articulates what the organization does to protect your information. You have not yet provided any personal information. What is this called?

Answers:

A. Opt-Out
B. Opt-In
C. Just-in-time-notice
D. Privacy Policy

Question 57.

Your organization distributed commercial electronic mail messages to consumers. One of the recipients requests the information covered in Art. 22(1) of GDPR. What information are they requesting?

Answers:

A. Purpose of the processing
B. Categories of personal data concerned
C. The existence of automated decision-making, including profiling
D. Any available information as to their source of information gathered

Question 58.

Your customer's information and their rights to control what and who collects their information, where their information is shared are privacy rights. What overlap is there with information security that relates to accountability?

Answers:

A. Availability
B. Confidentiality
C. Integrity
D. Accountability

Question 59.

A fundamental part of securing your organization's information as knowing what data you have and who can access it. It's the process of identifying and assigning predetermined levels of sensitivity to different types of information.

This not only means understanding what types of data you own, but what you're doing with it. For example, your organization is a financial institution which holds a person's mortgage application, which contains a wealth of Non-Public Personal Information (NPPI) like income level, current home address, their previous home address, other loan information, and more.

This information needs to be protected. What type of assessment must be conducted to determine the risks associated with the processing of this data?

A. Privacy Assessment
B. Privacy Impact Assessment
C. Data Protection Impact Assessment
D. Rule-based Assessment

Question 60.

An organization has shared objectives with other companies pertaining to the processing of data. As you continue to gather more information on all data processing activities, you also discover that you are processing the data for the same reason as another controller.
The data inventory is now complete along with each data processing activity for all data collected, and you determine that you are utilizing the same set of personal data for the processing as another controller.
What type of organization are you?

Answers:

A. Processing of data
B. Processor
C. Controller
D. Joint controller

Question 61.

Your organization utilizes both the Internet and email within your business. The following are requirements you must comply with if you distribute commercial messages, not only bulk emails:

- Online information services
- Online selling of products and services
- Online advertising
- Professional services
- Entertainment services and basic intermediary services

Which framework are these requirements from?

Answers:

A. Directive of Electronic Commerce
B. Directive on Privacy and Electronic Communications
C. Data Protection Directive
D. General Data Protection Regulation

Question 62.

In the United States, the federal government's approach to data privacy is a sector-based one. Data created with your organization's assets are your organization's property. Organizations generally transfer and use the data without notifying or gaining consent from the data subject.

The E.U., on the other hand, views data privacy as a human rights issue and guarantees the right to privacy in the European Convention for the Protection of Human Rights and Fundamental Freedoms.

You are the privacy professional of this multinational organization that has globalized business transactions and you must determine if your organization has suffered a cyber-attack. What type of action will you utilize to assist in that effort?

Answers:

A. Cross-Border Transfer
B. Intrastate Transfer
C. Interstate Transfer
D. e-Discovery Investigation

Question 63.

Your organization creates and protects its proprietary data that is being shared across organizations. There is a need to document which organization will be responsible for releasing data and what role the other organization(s) should take in assisting with that release.
There is a need to document the acceptable use of preliminary or provisional data by a partner or collaborator, as well.
One or more of the organizations requires what?

Answers:

A. BCR
B. SCC
C. Information Flow Map
D. Data Sharing Agreement

Question 64.

Your organization has completed its data inventory and data retention policy has been compiled to overlay the data within the organization's possession.

As outlined in the GDPR, data destruction — designated as the elimination, erasure or clearing of digital content — is classified as a form of data processing. It also means any destruction procedures should follow the specific rules set forth by the regulation. Here are three steps that need to be followed:

Step 1: Step one is obviously to implement the appropriate controls allowing data owners full rights and permissions over their affected content. Companies must provide users with an option to delete all personal data — including sales or browsing histories. It absolutely must be a practical option that stems the flow of new content and eliminates the old as soon as possible.

Step 2: Businesses are also obligated to ensure old data or content is securely erased. Just deleting it via the operating system or server is not enough. In fact, reformatting old drives and magnetic media — including hard drives or audio tapes — is no guarantee, either. Deleted data can often be recovered provided the physical media is available.

Step 3: It's important to properly dispose of?

Answers:

A. Hardware
B. Software
C. Records
D. Cloud storage

Question 65.

An organization that suffers a cyber event may be investigated to determine if they had the appropriate policies and procedures in place, along with documented training for their workforce. If the organization had those correct controls in place, this organization is able to prove that they have?

A. Consumer Trust
B. Compliance
C. Accountability
D. Responsibility

Question 66.

Article 51 of GDPR states that each Member State shall provide for one or more independent public authority to be responsible for monitoring the application of this Regulation, in order to protect the fundamental rights and freedoms of natural persons in relation to processing and to facilitate the free flow of personal data within the Union.

What authority is this?

Answers:

A. Data Protection Officer
B. Member of the EDPB
C. European Data Protection Supervisor
D. Supervisory authority

Question 67.

Whose core tasks are to supervise the EU institutions to help them be exemplary; public authorities must be beyond reproach when they process personal information.

We do this by monitoring those activities that use (process) personal data or information. The personal data could be yours or that of anyone else who works for or with the EU, including visitors, contractors or beneficiaries of grants.

Answers:

A. Supervisory authority
B. Data protection authority
C. Data protection officer
D. European Data Protection Supervisor

Question 68.

Under which GDPR article does it articulate that any person who has suffered material or non-material damage as a result of an infringement of this Regulation shall have the right to receive compensation from the controller or processor for the damage suffered.

Answers:

A. Art. 80
B. Art. 77
C. Art. 78
D. Art. 82

Question 69.

You, a citizen of a Member State, discovers and confirms that your information that is stored with a controller is incorrect. Which GDPR article provides you the right to rectify that discrepancy?

Answers:

A. Art. 16
B. Art. 15
C. Art. 17
D. Art. 19

Question 70.

As you assess your prospective processor, what is one topic that is not a priority for you to assess?

Answers:

A. Appropriate technical and organizational measures
B. Processor shall not engage another processor without specific or general written authorization
C. Processing by a processor shall be governed by a contract
D. What data the processor will process

Question 71.

You are making a purchase on an e-commerce website and a banner at the bottom of the page appears before you can provide your billing and shipping information. This banner articulates what the organization does to protect your information. What is this called?

Answers:

A. Opt-Out
B. Opt-In
C. Privacy Notice
D. Privacy Policy

Question 72.

Your multinational organization has voluntarily joined and started sharing cybersecurity information with other entities, both public and private within the United States of America. The sharing consists of cyber threat information while protecting classified information, intelligence sources and methods, and privacy and civil liberties.
This sharing of information authorizes companies to monitor and implement defensive measures on their own information systems to counter cyber threats. Second, it provides certain protections to encourage companies voluntarily to share information—specifically, information about "cyber threat indicators" and "defensive measures"—with the federal government, state and local governments, and other companies and private entities. These protections include protections from liability, non-waiver of privilege, and protections from FOIA disclosure, although, importantly, some of these protections apply only when sharing with certain entities.
What Act is this?

Answers:

A. Freedom of Information Act
B. Cybersecurity Information Sharing Act
C. Electronic Communications Privacy Act
D. Federal Trade Commission Act

Question 73.

You are reviewing your data inventory and determining what characteristics of data have been compiled that create a profile of the data subject. You have reviewed the GDPR, its recitals and definitions of data subjects.
All of the following are definitions of data subjects except?

Answers:

A. Resident of the EU
B. Personal data
C. Citizen of the EU
D. An EU Resident/Citizen located anywhere

Question 74.

As you and your organization review and assess prospective vendors/processors, you review data sharing implications, adequacy decisions, data subject's rights and appropriate technical and organizational measures.
Which of the following are not privacy matters to consider?

Answers:

A. Geographical location
B. Global Privacy Regulations
C. Cross-border data sharing
D. Competitor's Privacy Strategy

Question 75.

Data protection and safety is one of the most important things your organization can do if it regularly processes personal data.
Many provisions and stipulations of the GDPR boil down to a simple requirement: ensure the data is safe.
If you manage to do that, you have much less to worry about and all other issues that may arise become a lot easier to solve.
The following are all essential data protection methods except?

Answers:

A. Backups
B. Regulations
C. Pseudonymization
D. Encryption

Question 76.

Data subject rights are never absolute. There are conditions and exceptions, but there are also other rights to keep in mind. The right of freedom of expression and information, for instance, can have an impact with regards to the right of erasure.
You're providing an online newsletter. Your client gives their consent to subscribe to the online newsletter that allows you to process all the data on their interests to build a profile of what articles they consult. One year on, they inform you that they no longer wish to receive the online newsletter.
What must your organization do?

Answers:

A. Delete information
B. Remove from newsletter mailing list
C. Request consent again
D. Disclose information collected

Question 77.

You are consulting with your information security team on new lifecycle processes.
You are promoting the incorporation of data protection via their technology designs and
infrastructure implementations.
You remember that you can have security without privacy, however, you cannot have privacy
without security.
What design model is this referencing?

Answers:

A. Privacy by Default
B. Privacy by Design
C. Integrity and Confidentiality
D. Privacy Program

Question 78.

Your organization is a public authority that processes data and the core activities of the organization consist of processing operations whose scope and purposes require regular and systematic monitoring of data subjects on a large scale.

What does your organization need to designate?

Answers:

A. A Processor
B. A Controller
C. Data Protection Officer
D. A Judicial body

Question 79.

GDPR introduces in Article 5(2) GDPR the principle of accountability. According to this principle, the controller shall be responsible for compliance with the principles listed in Article 5(1) GDPR and addressed above and shall be able to what?

Answers:

A. Demonstrate compliance
B. Implement confidentiality and availability
C. Implement Privacy Notices
D. Implement Privacy Policies

Question 80.

You have been in your privacy professional role with your organization for just over one year. You are preparing for your first formal audit of the privacy program. What step of the five-phase audit cycle is this?

Answers:

A. First
B. Second
C. Third
D. Fourth

Question 81.

Which data principle is meaning that it is required to ensure that personal data are accurate and are kept up to date where it is necessary? Personal data that are inaccurate – considering the purposes for their processing – must be deleted or rectified without any delay?

Answers:

A. Proportional
B. Purpose limitation
C. Accuracy
D. Storage limitation

Question 82.

You have been in your privacy professional role with your organization for just over one year. You have finalized the research, materials and submitted the findings to your organization for their review. What step of the five-phase audit cycle is this?

Answers:

A. First
B. Second
C. Third
D. Fourth

Question 83.

Your organization is finalizing both the privacy policy and the information security policy. They are both drastically different, to include the structure to how they are presented and available for consumption.
They are both presented in with a layered approach. One of them is defining three levels. The top layer is a high-level document containing the controller's policy statement. The next layer is a more detailed document that sets out the security controls that will be implemented to achieve the policy statements. The third layer is the most detailed and contains the operating procedures, which explain how the policy statements will be achieved in practice.
Which policy are we discussing?

Answers:

A. Privacy Policy
B. Information Security Policy
C. Integrity Policy
D. Privacy Notice (layered)

Question 84.

Ransomware attacks continue to thrive on organizations globally and your organization has determined to become a more resilient organization.
Access controls and verification of identities have become a focal point.
Your information security group has determined to implement a new authentication process that requires more than one verification method. What is this security control called?

Answers:

A. Username and password
B. Tokenization
C. Encryption
D. Multi-factor authentication

Question 85.

GDPR addresses everything from data collection and sharing to data destruction. As part of respecting the rights of data owners, companies must also provide them with the option to wipe or delete any information in full. This is designated as the "right to be forgotten," or the right to erasure.
After your company has deleted the information, you discover residual magnetism is left behind. What is this called?

Answers:

A. Remanence
B. Deleted file
C. Disposal
D. Residual risk

Question 86.

A fair information practices principle, it is the principle stating there should be limits to the collection of personal data, that any such data should be obtained by lawful and fair means and, where appropriate, with the knowledge or consent of the data subject. This is called what?

Answers:

A. Collection limitation
B. Purpose limitation
C. Consent
D. Storage limitation

Question 87.

There are four classes of privacy that your organization must understand and control. One of those classes encompasses protection of the means of correspondence, including postal mail, telephone conversations, electronic e-mail and other forms of communicative behavior and apparatus.

Which class is this?

Answers:

A. Information privacy
B. Bodily privacy
C. Territorial privacy
D. Communications privacy

Question 88.

There are four classes of privacy that your organization must understand and control. One of those classes is to know when, how and to what extent information about them is communicated to others.
Which class is this?

Answers:

A. Information privacy
B. Bodily privacy
C. Territorial privacy
D. Communications privacy

Question 89.

There are four classes of privacy that your organization must understand and control. One of those classes concerns the setting of limits on intrusion into the domestic and other environments such as the workplace or public space. This includes searches, video surveillance and ID checks.
Which class is this?

Answers:

A. Information privacy
B. Bodily privacy
C. Territorial privacy
D. Communications privacy

Question 90.

There are four classes of privacy that your organization must understand and control. One of those classes focuses on a person's physical being and any invasion thereof. Such an invasion can take the form of genetic testing, drug testing or body cavity searches.

Which class is this?

Answers:

A. Information privacy
B. Bodily privacy
C. Territorial privacy
D. Communications privacy

Answer Key:

1. B	41. A	81. C
2. A	42. C	82. D
3. B	43. D	83. B
4. C	44. A	84. D
5. D	45. A	85. A
6. B	46. D	86. A
7. B	47. B	87. D
8. A	48. B	88. A
9. D	49. D	89. C
10. C	50. C	90. B
11. D	51. B	
12. C	52. D	
13. D	53. B	
14. A	54. D	
15. A	55. A	
16. D	56. C	
17. C	57. C	
18. D	58. D	
19. B	59. C	
20. B	60. D	
21. B	61. A	
22. D	62. D	
23. A	63. D	
24. B	64. A	
25. D	65. C	
26. B	66. D	
27. C	67. D	
28. B	68. D	
29. D	69. A	
30. C	70. D	
31. C	71. C	
32. D	72. B	
33. C	73. B	
34. C	74. D	
35. C	75. B	
36. B	76. A	
37. A	77. B	
38. C	78. C	
39. B	79. A	
40. D	80. B	

Question 1.

General Data Protection Law (LGPD) is Brazil's first comprehensive data protection law and is designed to enhance the privacy and protection of personal data of individuals in Brazil. The LGPD heavily resembles the EU General Data Protection Regulation (GDPR).

On September 17, 2020, the Brazilian president approved the bill, resulting in the LGPD taking effect on September 18, 2020.

At the end of October 2020, India announced that they are currently working towards a privacy regulation, similar, yet possibly more stringent than GDPR? What will this new law be named?

Answers:
A. General Data Protection Regulation (GDPR)
B. Personal Data Protection Act (PDPA)
C. Privacy Data Protection Act (PrDPA)
D. Personal Privacy Rights Act (PPRA)

The correct answer is B. The proposed naming convention of the Indian privacy regulation is Personal Data Protection Act (PDPA).
Answer C and D are distractors.

Question 2.

As the privacy professional of an investment organization, you are providing guidance and review of processes for collecting and processing of personal data collected from your employees.
GDPR Article 88 specifies there are more legislative layers applied and that can be imposed by Member States on what can be collected, when it can be collected and how it is collected and processed. All of the answers below are possible bases for processing personal information. Which one is not a preferred method?

As the privacy professional of an investment organization, you are providing guidance and review of <u>processes</u> for <u>collecting</u> and <u>processing</u> of <u>personal data</u> collected from your <u>employees.</u>
GDPR Article 88 specifies there are more legislative layers applied and that can be imposed by Member States on what can be collected, when it can be collected and how it is collected and processed. All of the answers below are possible bases for processing personal information. Which one is <u>not</u> a <u>preferred</u> method?

Key words: processes; collecting; processing; personal data; employees; not; preferred.

Questions to ask yourself – What is the question asking me or not asking me for?

Which one of the answers below is not preferred for processing data OF employees?

Answers:

A. Consent
B. Contract
C. Legitimate Interest
D. Legal Obligations

The correct answer is A. When talking about consent given under the employee-employer relationship, it is very difficult to obtain proper consent that is freely given, specific, informed and unambiguous, especially because given the relationship, there is an uneven distribution of power.
Can consent truly be given freely in an employee-employer relationship? If an employee wants to deny the employer of his/her consent, there is always a possibility that the employee might think about possible repercussions of that action. This can affect employees to give consent to avoid unpleasant situations or being in bad terms with an employer.
The best thing to do in those situations, from the employer's point of view, is to avoid consent as a legal base for processing. If an employer is a public authority, then consent is never appropriate considering the uneven distribution of power.

Question 3.

Privacy professionals are charged with the protection and appropriate use of?

Answers:

A. Private Information
B. Personal Information
C. Public Information
D. Social Information

The correct answer is B. The term Private Information is rarely utilized, while Personal Information (PI)and Personally Identifiable Information (PII) are predominantly used. PPs are not responsible for protecting either public information or social information. Do not read into the questions. Focus on the question as it is posed. If you imply or apply additional thoughts to the question, you may over think the question and choose the incorrect answer.

Question 4.

On July 16, 2020, the European Union Court of Justice (CJEU) invalidated the EU-US Privacy Shield in its decision in Facebook Ireland v. Schrems (Schrems II). The court determined that the Privacy Shield transfer mechanism does not comply with the level of protection required under EU law.
The decision reinforces the European Union's commitment to protecting what?

On July 16, 2020, the European Union Court of Justice (CJEU) invalidated the EU-US Privacy Shield in its decision in Facebook Ireland v. Schrems (Schrems II). The court determined that the Privacy Shield transfer mechanism does not comply with the level of protection required under EU law.
The decision reinforces the European Union's commitment to protecting what?

Key words: European Union Court of Justice; invalidated; EU-US Privacy Shield; transfer mechanism; not comply; level of protection

Questions to ask yourself – What is being transferred? What did the EU-US Privacy Shield provide organizations?

Answers:

A. Regulations
B. Security
C. Privacy
D. Citizens

The correct answer is C. The full answer would be the privacy of member's data. Answer D is incorrect. Had the question been presented differently around protecting an individual and not discussing Privacy Shield and levels of protection, perhaps then, answer D might have been a possible answer.
You will see questions that infer information that you must draw from and piece together for the correct answer on your actual exam. If you knew what Privacy Shield was and why it was created, you would then understand that protecting members' data privacy would be key.

Question 5.

Technologies that enable and enhance and preserve privacy and security of data throughout its entire lifecycle while protecting information privacy by eliminating or minimizing personal data is called?

Technologies that enable and enhance and preserve privacy and security of data throughout its entire lifecycle while protecting information privacy by eliminating or minimizing personal data is called?

Key words: Technologies; preserve privacy; data; lifecycle; information privacy; eliminating; minimizing personal data

Questions to ask yourself – What technologies preserve privacy/data?; What is information lifecycle (term)? What does minimizing personal data mean?

Answers:

A. Confidentiality
B. Data Protection
C. Information Security
D. Privacy Enabling Technologies

The correct answer is D. Privacy Enabling Technologies (PET) are tools that simply enable privacy. PETs fall under the paradigm of Privacy by Design (PbD) and within the privacy engineering discipline.

Question 6.

A framework approved by the European Union and US Government for complying with EU data protection regulations when data is transferred between the European Economic Area (EEA) and the United States is called?

Answers:

A. General Data Protection Regulation
B. Privacy Shield
C. Standard Contractual Clause
D. Binding Corporate Rules

The correct answer is B. The Privacy Shield is a framework approved by the European Union and US government for complying with EU data protection requirements. The General Data Protection Regulation (GDPR) is the toughest privacy and security law in the world, but does not mention the Privacy Shield within it, however, it does discuss international data transfers, adequacy decisions and data protection of EU member's data.

Question 7.

This institution consists of 705 members, seven political groups, 27 committees that the members participate in to prepare the work for plenary sessions. This institution is the EU's only directly elected institution. What institution is this?

Answers:

A. Council of Europe
B. European Parliament
C. European Commission
D. European Council

The correct answer is B. The European Parliament is the EU's only directly elected institution.

Answer A, the Council of Europe, is the continent's leading human rights organization, which includes 47 member states, 27 of which are members of the European Union.

Answer C, the European Commission, is the EU's politically independent executive arm. It is alone responsible for drawing up proposals for new European legislation, and it implements the decisions of the European Parliament and the Council of the EU.

Answer D, the European Council, The European Council defines the EU's overall political direction and priorities. It is not one of the EU's legislating institutions, so it does not negotiate or adopt EU laws. Instead it sets the EU's policy agenda, traditionally by adopting 'conclusions' during European Council meetings which identify issues of concern and actions to take.

Question 8.

Members of this institution are the heads of state or government of the 27 EU member states and the President of the European Commission. It is not one of the EU's legislating institutions, so it does not negotiate or adopt EU laws.
Instead, it sets the EU's policy agenda, traditionally by adopting 'conclusions' during its meetings which identify issues of concern and actions to take. What institution is this?

Answers:

A. European Council
B. European Parliament
C. European Commission
D. Council of Europe

The correct answer is A. The European Council defines the EU's overall political direction and priorities. It is not one of the EU's legislating institutions, so it does not negotiate or adopt EU laws. Instead it sets the EU's policy agenda, traditionally by adopting 'conclusions' during European Council meetings which identify issues of concern and actions to take.

Answer B, the European Parliament, is the EU's only directly elected institution.

Answer C, the European Commission, is the EU's politically independent executive arm. It is alone responsible for drawing up proposals for new European legislation, and it implements the decisions of the European Parliament and the Council of the EU.

Answer D, the Council of Europe, is the continent's leading human rights organization, which includes 47 member states, 27 of which are members of the European Union.

Question 9.

You are a resident of a multifamily housing complex and have provided personally identifiable information (PII) to the property management member to tour the complex and available units for possible leasing.
Upon returning to the office, you are provided with either a paper application or a web URL and link to complete and submit an electronic application. The questions are the same on both applications. You complete the application and alert the office representative that you have completed your application.
 The office representative begins to review the application and receives approval of your application.
To continue the process and to secure the unit, you are asked to provide more PII that includes your banking information that will be automatically debited on the 1st day of each month for your rent and utilities and a link to a complex website where you can share information, request maintenance and other information.
The property management team is GDPR compliant and provides you with your rights as a data subject. Which of the following are not one of those rights?

Answers:

A. Access
B. Rectification
C. Erasure and the right to be forgotten
D. Right to share

The correct answer is D. Right to share is not a listed data subject right. Section 1, Art. 12, Section 2, Art. 13-15, Section 3, Art. 16-20, Section 4, Art., 21-22, and Section 5, Art. 23 of the GDPR will provide more insight on the data subject rights.

Access – Art. 15
Rectification – Art. 16
Erasure and the right to be forgotten – Art. 17

Question 10.

You are a Data Protection Officer (DPO) for a multinational manufacturing organization. You have been in your current role for over 90 days. As part of your role, you have established a working relationship with your Data Protection Authority (DPA).
The DPA discusses matters with other DPA's and supports the cooperation between the EU's DPA's.
The EU's DPA's consistently apply data protection rules throughout the EU, which are contributed to by an independent European body that is composed of representatives of the national data protection authorities. The supervisory authorities of the EFTA EEA States are also members with regard to the GDPR related matters and without the right to vote and being elected as chair or deputy chairs. This Body is established by the General Data Protection Regulation (GDPR) and is based in Brussels. What is this body?

Answers:

A. European Council
B. European Data Protection Authority
C. European Data Protection Board
D. European Data Protection Supervisory

The correct answer is C. The European Data Protection Board (EDPB) is an independent European body, which contributes to the consistent application of data protection rules throughout the European Union and promotes cooperation between the EU's data protection authorities.

Answer A, the European Council, defines the EU's overall political direction and priorities. It is not one of the EU's legislating institutions, so it does not negotiate or adopt EU laws. Instead it sets the EU's policy agenda, traditionally by adopting 'conclusions' during European Council meetings which identify issues of concern and actions to take.

Answer B is wrong and does not exist.

Answer D is The European Data Protection Supervisor (EDPS) is the European Union's (EU) independent data protection authority. They monitor, advise, intervene and cooperate with national supervisory authorities.

Question 11.

Your organization is coordinating a cross-border effort and is working with the Global Privacy Enforcement Network (GPEN) prior to executing the transfer of data. Which one of the following agencies is not a part of the GPEN?

Answers:

A. European Data Protection Supervisor (EDPS)
B. Federal Commissioner for Data Protection and Freedom of Information
C. Information Commissioner's Office (ICO)
D. Office of Civil Rights

The correct answer is D. Answers A, B, and C are all members of GPEN.

For the complete listing of agencies, please check here.
https://www.privacyenforcement.net/authorities-listings

Question 12.

You are the privacy officer for a small healthcare organization that is conducting a self-regulatory self-assessment questionnaire (SAQ). Which one of these would this report best support?

Answers:

A. GDPR
B. EU Directive on Electronic Commerce
C. PCI DSS
D. U.S. HIPAA

The correct answer is C. Payment Card Industry Data Security Standard (PCI-DSS) is not a law or regulation. It's a standard that the four major credit card companies have adopted that tells merchants, essentially, if you want to collect payments from customers using credit and debit cards you must adhere to the PCI standard.
The European Union Agency for Cybersecurity, ENISA, is the Union's agency dedicated to achieving a high common level of cybersecurity across Europe. Established in 2004 and strengthened by the EU Cybersecurity Act, the European Union Agency for Cybersecurity contributes to EU cyber policy, enhances the trustworthiness of ICT products, services and processes with cybersecurity certification schemes, cooperates with Member States and EU bodies, and helps Europe prepare for the cyber challenges of tomorrow.
The European Union Agency for Cybersecurity considers the PCI-DSS standard a corporate governance item.

Question 13.

A Germany based organization receives its first data subject access request (DSAR). You are the privacy professional for the organization and are alerted to the receipt of the request in a timely fashion. What will you, as the privacy professional, reference, that was developed in the establishment of the privacy program, that will assist in determining where the DSAR's information resides?

Answers:

A. Data Classification Policy
B. Privacy Program Scope
C. Regulatory Map
D. Data Inventory

The correct answer is D. The data inventory will provide the PP with the source, types, uses, information flow path, storage, and other applicable data fields to start the collection of the SAR form.

Question 14.

This milestone document in the history of human rights was drafted by representatives with different legal and cultural backgrounds from all regions of the world, the Declaration was proclaimed by the United Nations General Assembly in Paris on 10 December 1948 (General Assembly resolution 217 A) as a common standard of achievements for all peoples and all nations. It sets out, for the first time, fundamental human rights to be universally protected and it has been translated into over 500 languages. What milestone is this?

Answers:

A. The Universal Declaration of Human Rights
B. The Declaration of the Rights of Man and of the Citizen
C. The United States Declaration of Independence
D. The Magna Carta

The correct answer is A. Also called the Human Rights Declaration, the declaration recognized the universal values and traditions of inherent dignity, freedom, justice and peace.

1215: The Magna Carta—gave people new rights and made the king subject to the law.

1628: The Petition of Right—set out the rights of the people.

1776: The United States Declaration of Independence—proclaimed the right to life, liberty and the pursuit of happiness.

1789: The Declaration of the Rights of Man and of the Citizen—a document of France, stating that all citizens are equal under the law.

Question 15.

Effective on May 25, 2018, this regulation is viewed as the toughest privacy and security law in the world. Though it was drafted and passed by the European Union (EU), it imposes obligations onto organizations anywhere, so long as they target or collect data related to people in the EU. This regulation levies harsh fines against those who violate its privacy and security standards, with penalties reaching into the tens of millions of euros, as we have seen from multiple organizations. Which regulation is this?

Answers:

A. General Data Protection Regulation
B. EU Directive on Electronic Commerce
C. EU Directive on Privacy and Electronic Communication
D. EU Data Protection Directive

The correct answer is A. The GDPR was effective on May 25, 2018.

Answer B was implemented in 2000. On 8 June 2000, the EU adopted the landmark 'electronic commerce' directive, a legal framework for the development of information society services.

Answer C was implemented in 2002. Directive 2002/58 on Privacy and Electronic Communications, otherwise known as the ePrivacy Directive, safeguards the confidentiality of electronic communications in the EU. The ePrivacy Directive is a key instrument to protect privacy and it includes specific rules on data protection in the area of telecommunication in public electronic networks. The directive was adopted in 2002 with the aim to address the requirements of new digital technologies.

Answer D was implemented in 1995. The "Directive 95/46 of the European Parliament and the Council of 24 October 1995 on the protection of individuals with regard to the processing of personal data and on the free movement of such data" (Data Protection Directive 95/46/EC) was established to provide a regulatory framework to guarantee secure and free movement of personal data across the national borders of the EU member countries, in addition to setting a baseline of security around personal information wherever it is stored, transmitted or processed. The Directive contains 33 articles in 8 chapters.

Question 16.

Given that children merit specific protection, any information and communication, where processing is addressed to a child, should be in such a clear and plain language that the child can easily understand. This represents which principle?

Answers:

A. Privacy Notice
B. Children's Online Privacy Protection Act
C. Purpose Limitation
D. Transparency principle

The correct answer is D. The principle of transparency requires that any information addressed to the public or to the data subject be concise, easily accessible and easy to understand, and that clear and plain language and, additionally, where appropriate, visualization be used.

Answer A is a statement made to a data subject that describes how the organization collects, uses, retains and discloses personal information. A privacy notice is sometimes referred to as a privacy statement, a fair processing statement or sometimes a privacy policy. Special privacy notices are also mandated by specific laws such as GLBA and COPPA in the United States.

Answer B places parents in control over what information is collected from their young children online. The Rule was designed to protect children under age 13, while accounting for the dynamic nature of the Internet.

Answer C is that personal data should not be disclosed, made available or otherwise used for purposes other than those specified in accordance with [the Purpose Specification Principle] except: (a) with the consent of the data subject; or (b) by the authority of law.

Question 17.

You are drafting a statement that is a public document which identifies who the data controller is, with contact details for its Data Protection Officer, which is you. It should also explain the purposes for which personal data are collected and used, how the data are used and disclosed, how long it is kept, and the controller's legal basis for processing.
What is this statement named?

Answers:

A. Privacy Statement
B. Privacy Policy
C. Privacy Notice
D. GDPR Notice

The correct answer is C. A privacy notice is one of several documents required for GDPR compliance. However, whereas many are strictly internal, a GDPR statement is provided to customers and other interested parties, explaining how the organization processes their personal data.

Answer A is sometimes utilized in lieu of saying it is a privacy notice, however, the regulation states it is a privacy notice.

Answer B is an internal facing policy on how the organization handles and protects its data.

Answer D is incorrect.

Question 18.

What type of data is not considered to be personal data by the GDPR, as detailed in Article 4(1), and its collection and processing is governed by the GDPR. Article 3(2) states that, "This Regulation applies to the processing of personal data of data subjects who are in the Union."

Answers:

A. Geolocation
B. Online identifier
C. Economic
D. Historic

The correct answer is D. Art. 4(1) - 'personal data' means any information relating to an identified or identifiable natural person ('data subject'); an identifiable natural person is one who can be identified, directly or indirectly, in particular by reference to an identifier such as a name, an identification number, location data, an online identifier or to one or more factors specific to the physical, physiological, genetic, mental, economic, cultural or social identity of that natural person;

Question 19.

Your organization moved to a work-from-home (WfH) model in March 2020. During that time frame, before your employees began to return-to-work (RtW) your HR and facility directors reviewed guidelines on all monitoring of employees, ensuring that everyone was and would be safe as they returned to their offices and cubicles.
A new monitoring solution to ensure all RtW employees are wearing masks and keeping social distance is to record, without sound, the common areas and workplace areas of the workforce. What type of monitoring is this?

Answers:

A. Surveillance by public authorities
B. Video surveillance
C. Facial recognition
D. Biometrics

The correct answer is B. Video surveillance is a recording that does not capture sound and potentially can capture facial recognition and biometrics. It may also be called Closed-Circuit television (CCTV). Answer C and D are distractors.
Answer A is wrong.

Question 20.

Your organization operates a commercial website and online services that collect and maintain covered information from all of its consumers. Your organization is targeting a number of member states and their residents. Which one of these marketing terms defines this action?

Answers:

A. Telemarketing
B. Direct marketing
C. Online behavioral targeting
D. Web cookies

The correct answer is B. Direct marketing includes emails and text messages that are sent to a targeted consumer for a particular product or service provider, where communication is sent directly to the targeted individual that has had a profile created and is being sent personalized communications and advertisements.

Answer A is direct marketing of goods or services to potential customers over the telephone, internet, or fax.

Answer C is a method that allows advertisers and publishers to display relevant ads and marketing messages to users based on their web-browsing behavior.

Answer D is a small piece of data stored on the user's computer by the web browser while browsing a website.

Question 21.

The Council of Europe invited member states to sign this treaty, which is based on human rights declaration and is an international treaty to protect human rights and fundamental freedoms. This treaty applies only to member states. What treaty is this?

Answers:

A. UN Declaration of Human Rights
B. Convention for the Protection of Human Rights and Fundamental Freedoms
C. Universal Human Rights Declaration
D. Organization for Economic Co-Operation and Development

The correct answer is B. The Convention for the Protection of Human Rights and Fundamental Freedoms, better known as the European Convention on Human Rights, was signed in Rome (Italy) on 4 November 1950 by 12 member states of the Council of Europe and entered into force on 3 September 1953.

Answer A, and answer C, the Universal Declaration of Human Rights (UDHR), is a milestone document in the history of human rights. Drafted by representatives with different legal and cultural backgrounds from all regions of the world, the Declaration was proclaimed by the United Nations General Assembly in Paris on 10 December 1948 (General Assembly resolution 217 A) as a common standard of achievements for all peoples and all nations. It sets out, for the first time, fundamental human rights to be universally protected and it has been translated into over 500 languages, are the same. The words in the title are simply shifted.

Answer D, The Organization for Economic Co-operation and Development (OECD), is an international organization that works to build better policies for better lives. Our goal is to shape policies that foster prosperity, equality, opportunity and well-being for all. We draw on almost 60 years of experience and insights to better prepare the world of tomorrow.

Question 22.

This was the first legally binding international instrument in the field of data protection and was a defining moment in the development of European Data Protection law.

Answers:

A. UN Human Declarations Right
B. Data Protection Directive
C. General Data Protection Regulation
D. Convention 108

The correct answer is D. The Convention for the Protection of Individuals with regard to Automatic Processing of Personal Data (CETS No. 108) The Convention opened for signature on 28 January 1981 and was the first legally binding international instrument in the data protection field.

Answer A, the Universal Declaration of Human Rights (UDHR), is a milestone document in the history of human rights. Drafted by representatives with different legal and cultural backgrounds from all regions of the world, the Declaration was proclaimed by the United Nations General Assembly in Paris on 10 December 1948 (General Assembly resolution 217 A) as a common standard of achievements for all peoples and all nations. It sets out, for the first time, fundamental human rights to be universally protected and it has been translated into over 500 languages, are the same.

Answer B, adopted in 1995 by the European Union, the Data Protection Directive is officially known as Directive 95/46/EC on the protection of individuals with regard to the processing of personal data and on the free movement of such data. The Data Protection Directive is binding within the member states of the EU and regulates how personal data is collected and processed in the European Union.

Answer C, the General Data Protection Regulation (GDPR), is the toughest privacy and security law in the world. Though it was drafted and passed by the European Union (EU), it imposes obligations onto organizations anywhere, so long as they target or collect data related to people in the EU. The regulation was put into effect on May 25, 2018. The GDPR will levy harsh fines against those who violate its privacy and security standards, with penalties reaching into the tens of millions of euros.

Question 23.

A B2B website features their teams' direct email addresses and telephone numbers for inquiries.
In this situation, you would be allowed to use these contact details to contact the person if you were interested in using their services.
Is it still possible to contact the person to sell your services? If so, what contact information would you be able to use under GDPR?

Answers:

A. Business contact data
B. Personal contact data
C. Social networking services
D. Artificial Intelligence

The correct answer is A.   However, you would not be allowed to contact the person to sell your own services (as in cold contact). This would be seen as prospecting and using the data for purposes where no permission has been given by the individual concerned.
Using the provided information for any purpose other than that stated is prohibited under the GDPR.
It is still possible to contact the organization to sell your services, but the main contact number or general email address should be used as these are not considered to be personal data under GDPR.

Question 24.

User consent must be obtained from clear and affirmative actions. Access to online content cannot depend on a visitor's agreement to process their personal data. These are two key points of the recently updated guidelines of the European Data Protection Board on the concept of consent. The guidelines provide recommendations on existing consent practices and make it clear that cookie walls are not compliant with the General Data Protection Regulation.

Your organization is using consent mechanisms, which rely on the use of scrolling, swiping through the webpage or any other form of continued browsing.

The EDPB clarifies that scrolling, swiping or continued browsing do not constitute such unambiguous consent.

None of these activities above can be regarded as providing valid consent under the GDPR.

Access to internet services should not be conditional on the acceptance of cookies. The practice called "Cookie walls" blocks content and prevents users from accessing content unless they consent to certain what?

Answers:

A. Consent
B. Cookies
C. Access
D. Direct Marketing

The correct answer is B. A computer "cookie" is more formally known as an HTTP cookie, a web cookie, an Internet cookie, or a browser cookie. The name is a shorter version of "magic cookie," which is a term for a packet of data that a computer receives, then sends back without changing or altering it. No matter what it's called, a computer cookie consists of information. When you visit a website, the website sends the cookie to your computer. Your computer stores it in a file located inside your web browser.

Question 25.

Your organization is migrating their applications and processes to a cloud computing platform. Accessibility, storage and management are key business drivers for this effort.

All of the following are challenges in cloud computing within GDPR except?

Answers:

A. Data retention
B. Data processing outside of the EEA
C. Data ownership
D. Vendor management

The correct answer is D. All of the other answers are correct. Vendor management is not a part of cloud computing, however, selecting a vendor for cloud computing may be a challenge, but that is not what the question is asking you.

You will see questions similar to this ask and thought process on your exam.

Question 26.

Your customer's information and their rights to control what and who collects their information, where their information is shared are privacy rights. Which of the following is not one of the lawful processing criteria?

Answers:

A. Contractual necessity
B. Sensitive vital information
C. Legal obligations
D. Legitimate interest

The correct answer is B. GDPR provides six legal bases for processing:

Consent
Performance of a Contract
Legitimate Interest
Vital Interest
Legal Requirement
Public Interest

Question 27.

In 1996, the Department of Health and Human Services within the United States of America, signed into law the Healthcare Insurance Portability and Accountability Act (HIPAA). HIPAA was created to "improve the portability and accountability of health insurance coverage" for employees between jobs.
Within GDPR, Art. 20 empowers the data subject to have the right receive the personal data concerning him or her, which he or she has provided to a controller, in a structured, commonly used and machine-readable format and have the right to transmit those data to another controller without hindrance from the controller to which the personal data have been provided. This right is what?

A. Access
B. Rectification
C. Data portability
D. Automated decision making

The correct answer is C. Recital 68 also addresses the right of data portability. The right to data portability allows data subjects to obtain and reuse personal data about them for their own purposes across different services. It allows data subjects to move, copy or transfer personal data easily from one IT environment to another in a safe and secure way without affecting its usability. This enables data subjects to take advantage of different applications and services that can use their data to find them a better deal or help them understand their spending habits.
The right only applies to information about a data subject provided to a controller.

Question 28.

Your organization has conducted and inventoried all data flows, classifying the data elements and its flow, both internally and externally. All data within each lifecycle step have had physical, technical and administrative security controls applied to protect the confidentiality, integrity, and availability of that data.
What might be said about your organization's security measures implemented?

Answers:

A. Adequacy decision
B. Appropriate technical and organizational measures
C. Accuracy and storage
D. Storage limitation

The correct answer is B. Art. 32, Security of Processing, taking into account the state of the art, the costs of implementation and the nature, scope, context and purposes of processing as well as the risk of varying likelihood and severity for the rights and freedoms of natural persons, the controller and the processor shall implement appropriate technical and organizational measures to ensure a level of security appropriate to the risk.

Question 29.

Your organization encrypts and redacts the personal and business critical data it controls. Your organization suffers a data breach. After you have contacted your data breach coach and deploy a forensic investigator, it is determined that your encryption key has not been compromised. Based on Art. 33, who must you notify?

Answers:

A. Data Protection Authority
B. Supervisory Authority
C. Data Protection Officer
D. No one

The correct answer is D. A notification to a supervisory authority is not required if there is unlikely to be a risk to the rights and freedoms of individuals. The WP gives an example of where a securely encrypted mobile device is lost but the organization retains the encryption key and adequate backup copies of the lost data.

If the encryption key is compromised, the controller shall without undue delay and, where feasible, not later than 72 hours after having become aware of it notify the supervisory authority.

Question 30.

It is vital that employers view data protection as an obligation to safeguard their employee's personal data, which is also required under employment law and collective agreements with trade unions and other bodies.
In certain cases, processing activities that involve employee data also involves interacting with DPAs, where they may not approve processing unless and until who has been involved?

Answers:

A. HR
B. Legal
C. Work Councils
D. Employees

The correct answer is C. European Works Councils are bodies representing the European employees of a company. Through them, workers are informed and consulted by management on the progress of the business and any significant decision at European level that could affect their employment or working conditions.

Member States are to provide for the right to establish European Works Councils in companies or groups of companies with at least 1000 employees in the EU and the other countries of the European Economic Area (Norway, Iceland and Liechtenstein), when there are at least 150 employees in each of two Member States.

Question 31.

The GDPR demands clarity through a privacy notice. Your privacy notice must be concise, transparent, intelligible and easily accessible; written in clear and plain language, particularly if addressed to a child; and free of charge.
This means a simple link to your crazy-long privacy policy during registration will likely not do the trick.
What is the preferred method of providing your privacy notice to the public?

Answers:

A. Transparent
B. Short
C. Layered
D. Simple

The correct answer is C. Layered notices allow users to access easy-to-understand information and then delve more deeply if required. Privacy notices are the windows to how organizations collect, use, share, and protect the information that pertains to individuals.

Question 32.

As your organization decides on what data to collect, it must identify valid business purposes, known as a lawful basis, for collecting and using personal data. Art. 5(1) of the GDPR outlines six data protection principles. Which is the first?

Answers:

A. Purpose limitation
B. Data minimization
C. Accuracy
D. Fairness

The correct answer is D. The first principle concerns lawfulness, fairness and transparency. It requires that personal data are processed in a lawful, fair and transparent manner in relation to data subjects. Transparency implies that any information and communication concerning the processing of personal data must be easily accessible and easy to understand. Also, clear and plain language needs to be used in this regard. More specifically, this principle ensures data subjects receive information on the identity of controllers and purposes of the processing of personal data.

The second principle is that of purpose limitation.

As the third principle, we need to refer to data minimization.

Accuracy is the fourth principle meaning that it is required to ensure that personal data are accurate and are kept up to date where it is necessary.

The fifth principle is storage limitation.

Finally, the sixth principle of integrity and confidentiality requires that in the processing of personal data appropriate security of personal data is ensured.

In addition to the six data protection principles, the GDPR introduces in Article 5(2) GDPR the principle of accountability, without which they cannot be brought to life. According to this principle, the controller shall be responsible for compliance with the principles listed in Article 5(1) GDPR and addressed above and shall be able to demonstrate its compliance with them.

Question 33.

In which chronological order were the following frameworks adopted?

Answers:

A. Directive on Privacy and Electronic Communications/Data Protection Directive/Directive on Electronic Commerce/GDPR
B. Data Protection Directive/Directive on Privacy and Electronic Communications/Directive on Electronic Commerce/GDPR
C. GDPR/Directive on Privacy and Electronic Communications/Data Protection Directive/Directive on Electronic Commerce
D. Council 108/Data Protection Directive/Directive on Electronic Commerce/Directive on Privacy and Electronic Communications

The correct answer is D.   1981, 1995, 2000, and 2002. GDPR was adopted in 2018.

Question 34.

GDPR non-compliant fines are based on the specific articles of the Regulation that the organization has breached. Infringements of the organization's obligations, including data security breaches, will be subject to the lower level, whereas infringements of an individual's privacy rights will be subject to the higher level. Data controllers and processors face administrative fines of the higher of €10 million or 2% of annual global turnover for infringements of articles:
8 (conditions for children's consent),
11 (processing that doesn't require identification),
25-39 (general obligations of processors and controllers),
42 (certification), and
43 (certification bodies)

The higher of €20 million or 4% of annual global turnover for infringements of articles:
5 (data processing principles),
6 (lawful bases for processing),
7 (conditions for consent),
9 (processing of special categories of data),
12-22 (data subjects' rights), and
44-49 (data transfers to third countries).

In 2019, British Airways was fined what amount for a 2018 data breach over data security failings which enabled unauthorized access to be obtained to personal and payment card information relating to more than 500,000 of its customers.

Answers:

A. €10 million
B. €20 million
C. €183 million
D. €30 million

The correct answer is C. The $230 million fine (£183.4 million) is 1.5% of BA's global turnover for the year, its parent company International Airlines Group noted in a statement. Under GDPR, companies can be fined the equivalent of $22.4 million or 4% of their total annual worldwide revenue in the preceding financial year, whichever is higher.

Question 35.

Under Art. 82, Right to Compensation and Liability, a controller or processor shall be exempt from liability under para. 2 if it proves that it is not in any way responsible for the event giving rise to the what?

Answers:

A. Processing
B. Data Sharing
C. Damages
D. Cross-border transfers

The correct answer is C. Per Art. 82, any person who has suffered material or non-material damage as a result of an infringement of this Regulation shall have the right to receive compensation from the controller or processor for the damage suffered.

Para. 2 – (1) Any controller involved in processing shall be liable for the damage caused by processing which infringes this Regulation. (2) A processor shall be liable for the damage caused by processing only where it has not complied with obligations of this Regulation specifically directed to processors or where it has acted outside or contrary to lawful instructions of the controller.

Para. 3 - A controller or processor shall be exempt from liability under paragraph 2 if it proves that it is not in any way responsible for the event giving rise to the damage.

Question 36.

You are the privacy professional for your organization and are looking to apply data protection principles within your organization's processes.
As you review current processes, you determine that data processing is not being processed for the purposes they were collected for. Which principle do you need to implement?

Answers:

A. Purpose Limitation
B. Data Minimization
C. Accuracy
D. Storage Limitation

The correct answer is B. According to the Data Minimization principle, personal data must be adequate, relevant and limited to what is necessary in relation to the purposes for which they are processed. Essentially, it means that data cannot be processed unless it is needed to process them in order achieve the above-mentioned purposes.

Question 37.

Your organization relies on B2B sales, which is competitive by nature. Your sales teams cannot escape GDPR and its reach and regulations. You hold a sales team meeting to discuss the following
Do you still rely on purchased leads to fill up your sales pipeline?
Do you automatically add business card contact data to your mailing list?
Do you ask existing customers for referrals and recommendations?
If you answered "yes" to any of the questions above, then GDPR has an impact on you and your organization.
If you continue to solicit prospects to purchase your products or services, this is called?

Answers:

A. Telemarketing
B. Marketing
C. Email marketing
D. Social network marketing

The correct answer is A. Telemarketing is a method of direct marketing in which a salesperson solicits prospective customers to buy products or services, either over the phone or through a subsequent face to face or web conferencing appointment scheduled during the call.

Answer D, Social network marketing, is the use of social media platforms and websites to promote a product or service.

Question 38.

Your organization is a publicly traded investment company and data protection is critical to your operations. The impact of a successful data breach may have consequences that extend beyond your organization and impacts other market participants and retail investors, who may not be well informed of these risks and consequences.

Your organization has decided to repurpose data. You are reviewing the legitimate interest possibility for the repurposing and processing of personal data. You have conducted three tests to ensure your organization can utilize legitimate purposes for that processing. Two of those tests were the Necessity test and the Balancing of Interest test. What is the third test that must be met?

Answers:

A. Storage
B. Limitation
C. Purpose
D. Legitimate test

The correct answer is C. Processing is lawful if it:
"is necessary for the purposes of the legitimate interests pursued by the controller or by a third party, except where such interests are overridden by the interests or fundamental rights and freedoms of the data subject which require protection of personal data, in particular where the data subject is a child."
The purpose test asks you to consider whether you are processing personal data in pursuit of a legitimate interest. ... "Legitimate" means in-line with the data processing principles of the GDPR, and what your users would reasonably expect. "Interests" is used in the sense of a benefit.
Necessity is required to make sure that all possible considerations have been evaluated with respect to the need to use the data as intended. Are there alternative sources of data that are equally viable to achieve the same outcome?
Balancing of Interests is required to make sure the identity of individuals is protected and that as a result of the intended processing or subsequent failures in that processing, that it doesn't lead to a material risk of harm to the individuals concerned.

Question 39.

The Coronavirus has impacted the globe both personally and professionally. Initial reports in March and April 2020 had five new cases a day being reported in areas, which was viewed as high. On November 4, 2020, over 100k cases were reported in one day within the U.S.
What type of processing of personal data is this?

Answers:

A. Legitimate Interest
B. Public Interest
C. Consent
D. Contract

The correct answer is B. According to Article 9 (2) of the GDPR, sensitive data, including personal health-related data, can only be processed inter alia when data subject gives her/his explicit consent or when processing is necessary 'for reasons of public interest in the area of public health' on the basis of Union or Member State law.

Question 40.

This employment practice is an indispensable element of a functioning compliance management system. All companies with more than 50 employees as well as financial service providers and municipalities with more than 10,000 inhabitants will in future be obliged to set up these systems.
What type of system is this?

Answers:

A. Workplace monitoring
B. Storage
C. Retention
D. Whistleblowing system

The correct answer is D. Employee data protection in whistleblowing procedures inevitably leads to a conflict of interest between whistleblower protection and the right of the accused to information. Data protection in the context of internal whistleblower systems is like a combat zone. On the one hand, the protection of the whistleblower and the employer's interest in secrecy, on the other hand, the accused employee's interest in information. According to the EU Whistleblower Directive adopted on October 7, 2019, all companies with more than 50 employees as well as financial service providers and municipalities with more than 10,000 inhabitants will in future be obliged to set up whistleblower systems.

Question 41.

You are overall responsible for protecting the data of your organization. That includes business, personal, and employee' data. You need to have visibility to; where the data is, where it's going, and who has access. Network level visibility is fundamental to understanding these questions, but in an environment that allows personally owned devices, any visibility is lost the second the device walks out the door and outside your network.

Your organization is attempting to rectify this issue by making use of Enterprise Mobility Management (EMM) tools for application control and some device-level management, but neglect network level control. For a personal device, this makes sense. It's totally understandable that employees would refuse to install a solution that can see even just a scrap of their online activity. Device-level monitoring of an EMM is about as intrusive as most would allow and indicators of risk go overlooked as a result.

Corporate-owned and issued devices, on the other hand, have a greater degree of control and the script is pretty simple to communicate to employees – "we issue you the device, you use it in-line with corporate acceptable use policy and we monitor activity (the same as we would on your desktop) in order to keep our data safe from hackers". It's less simple when the device is owned by the employee. What type of model is this discussing?

Answers:

A. Bring Your Own Device (BYOD)
B. Shadow IT
C. Virtual Private Network (VPN)
D. IT Lifecycle

The correct answer is A. According to the General Data Protection Regulation (GDPR), the data controller must be in control of the data at all times, which is near impossible when the controller does not own the device where the data is being accessed or stored (i.e. in a BYOD model). BYOD is utilizing employee's personally owned devices for work purposes.

Question 42.

The Directive on Patients' Rights in Cross-Border Healthcare provides a legal basis for establishing a network on e-health in order to address such practical issues, focusing in particular on cross-border aspects (such as summary records for cross-border care, identification and secure sharing of information), as well as the vital strategic issue of methods for using e-health to enable use of medical information for public health and research – potentially an answer to address the delays that currently plague health data.

The European Commission also finances a wide range of projects developing and piloting e-health technologies and applications, for example in support of the European Innovation Partnership on Active and Healthy Ageing. E-health is presented as a way to address the shortage of health professionals in the European Union, to ensure better care of ageing populations and chronic diseases putting pressure on health budgets, as well as to remedy unequal quality and access to healthcare services in Europe.
Which Article of the GDPR addresses personal health information?

Answers:

A. Art. 4
B. Art. 5
C. Art. 9
D. Art. 11

The correct answer is C. Article 9, Processing of special categories of personal data is processing of personal data revealing racial or ethnic origin, political opinions, religious or philosophical beliefs, or trade union membership, and the processing of genetic data, biometric data for the purpose of uniquely identifying a natural person, data concerning health or data concerning a natural person's sex life or sexual orientation shall be prohibited.

Question 43.

Your organization is planning on cross-border transfers from the EU to the U.S. You are working on creating internal rules which define international policy within your multinational organization. What codes of conduct are you creating?

Answers:

A. External codes of conduct for cross-border transfers
B. Internal data protection training
C. Standard Contractual Clauses
D. Binding Corporate Rules

The correct answer is D. Binding Corporate Rules or BCRs are internal rules which define the international policy in a multinational group of companies and international organizations regarding intra-organizational personal data cross-border transfers.

Every entity acting as data controller must be responsible for and able to demonstrate compliance with the BCRs. Binding Corporate Rules are strict and approved codes of conduct but not in the broadest sense of approved codes of conduct under the GDPR: they are internal codes of conduct which concern transfers of personal data to third countries in the context of cross-border data transfers to entities of the international organization or multinationals (a group of undertakings, or group of enterprises engaged in a joint economic activity, including members) which are outside the EU.

Question 44.

On July 16, 2020, the CJEU invalidated the E.U.-U.S. Privacy Shield, one of the methods for transfers of personal data into the U.S. The court found that under U.S. surveillance laws, the U.S. government has access to personal data that does not provide Europeans with privacy protections equivalent to those in the E.U.
Which answer below is most associated with this ruling?

Answers:

A. Schrems
B. Snowden
C. GDRP
D. Privacy Protection

The correct answer is A. The case stems from a complaint filed by privacy advocate Max Schrems with the Irish Data Protection Commissioner ("Irish DPA") in 2015, challenging Facebook Ireland's use of the SCCs to transfer personal data to Facebook Inc. in the U.S. Specifically, Schrems alleged that the SCCs do not ensure an adequate level of protection for EU data subjects, as U.S. legislation does not explicitly limit interference with an individual's right to protection of personal data in the same way as EU data protection law. A key concern was that EU personal data might be at risk of being accessed and processed by the U.S. government once transferred, in a manner incompatible with privacy rights guaranteed in the EU under the Charter of Fundamental Rights.

Accordingly, Schrems argued that there was no remedy allowing EU data subjects to ensure protection of their personal data once it had been transferred to the U.S. Following the complaint, the Irish DPA brought proceedings against Facebook in the Irish High Court, challenging the validity of the SCCs, and referring 11 questions to the CJEU for a preliminary ruling.

Question 45.

You are the privacy professional within your organization. Your organization processes personal data wholly or partly by automated means and the processing other than by automated means of personal data which do form part of a filing system or are intended to form a filing system applies to which GDPR article?

Answers:

A. Art. 2
B. Art. 3
C. Art. 1
D. Art. 4

The correct answer is A. Article 2 addresses Material scope.

Answer B, Article 3, addresses Territorial scope and the processing of personal data in the context of the activities of an establishment of a controller or a processor in the Union, regardless of whether the processing takes place in the Union or not.
This Regulation applies to the processing of personal data of data subjects who are in the Union by a controller or processor not established in the Union, where the processing activities are related to: the offering of goods or services, irrespective of whether a payment of the data subject is required, to such data subjects in the Union; or the monitoring of their behavior as far as their behavior takes place within the Union.
This Regulation applies to the processing of personal data by a controller not established in the Union, but in a place where Member State law applies by virtue of public international law.
Answer C addresses Subject-matter and objectives while Answer D addresses Definitions.

Question 46.

Your organization must share personal information to a country outside of the EEA and EU. You individually tailor the contract to your company's needs and obtain the required supervisory authority's authorization. What type of cross-border transfer rule are you using?

Answers:

A. BCR
B. SCC
C. Codes of Conduct
D. Ad hoc contractual clause

The correct answer is D. BCRs allow organizations to create an internal policy. SCCs (Article 46(c) and Codes of conduct (Article 40) are addressed with the GDPR with enforceable commitments.

Question 47.

You are the privacy professional within your organization. Your organization processes personal data of data subjects who are in the Union by a controller or processor not established in the Union, where the processing activities are related to the offering of goods or services. Which GDPR article applies?

Answers:

A. Art. 2
B. Art. 3
C. Art. 1
D. Art. 4

The correct answer is B. Article 3 addresses Territorial scope and the processing of personal data in the context of the activities of an establishment of a controller or a processor in the Union, regardless of whether the processing takes place in the Union or not.
This Regulation applies to the processing of personal data of data subjects who are in the Union by a controller or processor not established in the Union, where the processing activities are related to: the offering of goods or services, irrespective of whether a payment of the data subject is required, to such data subjects in the Union; or the monitoring of their behavior as far as their behavior takes place within the Union.
This Regulation applies to the processing of personal data by a controller not established in the Union, but in a place where Member State law applies by virtue of public international law.
Answer C addresses Subject-matter and objectives while Answer D addresses Definitions.

Question 48.

An individual is applying for a new, open position listed on a job board website, which is your organization's role. Your organization requires that in the processing of personal data appropriate security of personal data is ensured. This should include protection against unauthorized or unlawful processing, destruction and damage. Appropriate technical or organizational measures are to be taken in order to comply with this requirement: such data security measures can include the use of encryption and authentication and authorization mechanisms.

Which of the six data protection principles is this?

Answers:

A. Accountability
B. Integrity and Confidentiality
C. Security Controls
D. Data Minimization

The correct answer is B. All of these principles can be found in Art. 5(1) of GDPR.

Question 49.

When a data subject makes an online purchase, a controller processes the address of the individual in order to deliver the goods. Which of the six lawful bases for processing is this?

Answers:

A. Consent
B. Legitimate interest
C. Legal obligation
D. Contractual necessity

The correct answer is D. Article 6(1)(b) of the GDPR provides a lawful basis for the processing of personal data to the extent that the processing is: Necessary for the performance of a contract to which the data subject is a party; or. In order to take steps at the request of the data subject prior to entering into a contract.

Question 50.

Your organization completed the data inventory exercise. What term is explicitly highlighted in Article 6(4)(e) as an "appropriate safeguard" that can be used by data controllers "in order to ascertain whether processing for another purpose is compatible with the purpose for which the personal data are initially collected?

Answers:

A. Data minimization
B. Anonymize
C. Pseudonymization
D. Data encryption

The correct answer is C. Recital 28, Introduction of Pseudonymization, states that the application of pseudonymization to personal data can reduce the risks to the data subjects concerned and help controllers and processors to meet their data-protection obligations. The explicit introduction of 'pseudonymization' in this Regulation is not intended to preclude any other measures of data protection.

Question 51.

Which data protection principle entails that personal data must be kept in a form that makes it possible to identify data subjects for no longer than is necessary for the purposes of the processing. Keeping these data for longer periods is allowed when the processing of the data will aim at achieving purposes in the public interest, scientific or historical research purposes or statistical purposes. Nevertheless, also in these cases rights and freedoms of data subjects must be safeguarded.

Answers:

A. Purpose limitation
B. Storage
C. Integrity and Confidentiality
D. Accuracy

The correct answer is B. The fifth principle is storage limitation. It entails that personal data must be kept in a form that makes it possible to identify data subjects for no longer than is necessary for the purposes of the processing. Storing these data for longer periods is allowed when the processing of the data will aim at achieving purposes in the public interest, scientific or historical research purposes or statistical purposes. Nevertheless, also in these cases rights and freedoms of data subjects must be safeguarded.

Question 52.

GDPR does not prevent video monitoring even when the employee does not know or consent to being monitored. Labor unions and work councils may negotiate limitations on video recordings of unionized workers. Union members should speak with a union representative if they have concerns about workplace video monitoring.
Your organization requires these in order to monitor its workforce except?

Answers:

A. Vital interest
B. Public interest
C. Legitimate interest
D. Personal interest

The correct answer is D. All listed answers are correct, except for D.

Question 53.

Your organization processes and collects over 1,000,000 credit card transactions annually. You have conducted an assessment on your PCI-DSS compliance. The PCI-DSS deals strictly with payment card data and cardholder information, such as credit/debit card numbers, primary account numbers (PAN), and sensitive authentication data (SAD) such as CVVs and magnetic stripe data, from all the major card schemes.

The GDPR has a much wider scope and covers any personally identifiable information (PII). The type of data in scope for GDPR includes PII related to any EU resident, whether it is connected to his or her private, professional or public life. This can include a name, home address, photo, email address, bank details, medical information, posts on social networking websites, or a computer's IP address.
Your organization suffers a breach that violates PCI DSS compliance, which now, also, violates the GDPR.
Which data protection principle applies here?

Answers:

A. Data minimization
B. Integrity and Confidentiality
C. Storage limitation
D. Purpose limitation

The correct answer is B. The PCI-DSS establishes a set of controls for keeping cardholder data secure, supported by a regulatory framework. If deployed to the rest of the business – without extending the cardholder data environment – these same controls and processes could provide organizations with a head start in meeting the sixth principle of the GDPR (integrity and confidentiality). This principle requires data controllers and processors to assess risk, implement appropriate security for the data concerned and, crucially, check on a regular basis that it is up to date and that controls to protect it are working effectively.

Question 54.

Your organization is conducting a thorough review of all data processing activities executed by the organization.

All of the following were inventoried. Which one is not data processing?

Answers:

A. Shredding documents containing personal data
B. Sending promotional emails
C. Video recording
D. Posting information on its social network

The correct answer is D. Processing covers a wide range of operations performed on personal data, including by manual or automated means. It includes the collection, recording, organization, structuring, storage, adaptation or alteration, retrieval, consultation, use, disclosure by transmission, dissemination or otherwise making available, alignment or combination, restriction, erasure or destruction of personal data.

The General Data Protection Regulation (GDPR) applies to the processing of personal data wholly or partly by automated means as well as to non-automated processing, if it is part of a structured filing system.

Question 55.

You are receiving unsolicited text messages and calls from multiple political parties during the campaign season. You have contacted the organization that continues to contact you and have asked to be removed from their distribution list.
You then follow up that initial request with a request to have all of your personal data erased.
This right to erasure is also known as the right to be forgotten. How long does the organization have to respond to the request?

Answers:

A. 30 days
B. Without undue delay
C. 60 days
D. 31 days

The correct answer is A. You have one month to respond to this request. The right is not absolute and only applies in certain circumstances. You may review Art. 17 and Recitals 65 and 66 for more information.

Question 56.

You are making a purchase on an e-commerce website and you receive a notice in the middle of the page that articulates what the organization does to protect your information. You have not yet provided any personal information. What is this called?

Answers:

A. Opt-Out
B. Opt-In
C. Just-in-time-notice
D. Privacy Policy

The correct answer is C. The notice is provided to the customer before any information is collected and articulates how that information will be protected along with the consumer's choices and rights. It is an external statement. A privacy policy is an internal communication.

Question 57.

Your organization distributed commercial electronic mail messages to consumers. One of the recipients requests the information covered in Art. 22(1) of GDPR. What information are they requesting?

Answers:

A. Purpose of the processing
B. Categories of personal data concerned
C. The existence of automated decision-making, including profiling
D. Any available information as to their source of information gathered

The correct answer is C. Art. 22, Automated individual decision-making, including profiling, provides the data subject shall have the right not to be subject to a decision based solely on automated processing, including profiling, which produces legal effects concerning him or her or similarly significantly affects him or her.

Question 58.

Your customer's information and their rights to control what and who collects their information, where their information is shared, are privacy rights. What overlap is there with information security that relates to accountability?

Answers:

A. Availability
B. Confidentiality
C. Integrity
D. Accountability

The correct answer is D. Answers A, B and C are the information security triads. Accountability falls in both privacy and information security requiring data owners, controllers, and processors to protect the data adequately.

Question 59.

A fundamental part of securing your organization's information as knowing what data you have and who can access it. It's the process of identifying and assigning predetermined levels of sensitivity to different types of information.

This not only means understanding what types of data you own, but what you're doing with it. For example, your organization is a financial institution which holds a person's mortgage application, which contains a wealth of Non-Public Personal Information (NPPI) like income level, current home address, their previous home address, other loan information, and more.

This information needs to be protected. What type of assessment must be conducted to determine the risks associated with the processing of this data?

A. Privacy Assessment
B. Privacy Impact Assessment
C. Data Protection Impact Assessment
D. Rule-based Assessment

The correct answer is C. A data protection impact assessment must always be conducted when the processing could result in a high risk to the rights and freedoms of natural persons.

Answer A is an assessment of an organization's compliance with its privacy policies and procedures and applicable laws.

Answer B is an analysis of how information is handled.

Answer D is incorrect.

Question 60.

An organization has shared objectives with other companies pertaining to the processing of data. As you continue to gather more information on all data processing activities, you also discover that you are processing the data for the same reason as another controller.
The data inventory is now complete along with each data processing activity for all data collected, and you determine that you are utilizing the same set of personal data for the processing as another controller.
What type of organization are you?

Answers:

A. Processing of data
B. Processor
C. Controller
D. Joint controller

The correct answer is D. Your company/organization is a joint controller when together with one or more organizations it jointly determines 'why' and 'how' personal data should be processed. Joint controllers must enter into an arrangement setting out their respective responsibilities for complying with the GDPR rules.

Question 61.

Your organization utilizes both the Internet and email within your business. The following are requirements you must comply with if you distribute commercial messages, not only bulk emails:

- Online information services
- Online selling of products and services
- Online advertising
- Professional services
- Entertainment services and basic intermediary services

Which framework are these requirements from?

Answers:

A. Directive of Electronic Commerce
B. Directive on Privacy and Electronic Communications
C. Data Protection Directive
D. General Data Protection Regulation

The correct answer is A. The Directive sets out basic requirements on mandatory consumer information, steps to follow in online contracting and rules on commercial communications (e.g. online advertisement and unsolicited commercial communications). The Directive establishes harmonized rules on issues such as:
-transparency and information requirements for online service providers,
-commercial communications,
-electronic contracts and limitations of liability of intermediary service providers.

It also enhances administrative cooperation between the Member States and the role of self-regulation.

Question 62.

In the United States, the federal government's approach to data privacy is a sector-based one. Data created with your organization's assets are your organization's property. Organizations generally transfer and use the data without notifying or gaining consent from the data subject.

The E.U., on the other hand, views data privacy as a human rights issue and guarantees the right to privacy in the European Convention for the Protection of Human Rights and Fundamental Freedoms.

You are the privacy professional of this multinational organization that has globalized business transactions and you must determine if your organization has suffered a cyber-attack. What type of action will you utilize to assist in that effort?

Answers:

A. Cross-Border Transfer
B. Intrastate Transfer
C. Interstate Transfer
D. e-Discovery Investigation

The correct answer is D. You must understand what data you collect, use, share, store, and retain along with a flow path to overlay the appropriate security controls to protect the classification of that data, both internally and externally. Conducting an e-discovery investigation will capture that entire process, which may be utilized for DSAR or SAR, depending on where you are located.

Question 63.

Your organization creates and protects its proprietary data that is being shared across organizations. There is a need to document which organization will be responsible for releasing data and what role the other organization(s) should take in assisting with that release.
There is a need to document the acceptable use of preliminary or provisional data by a partner or collaborator, as well.
One or more of the organizations requires what?

Answers:

A. BCR
B. SCC
C. Information Flow Map
D. Data Sharing Agreement

The correct answer is D. Successful interagency data sharing and collaboration is based on adopting guiding principles, identifying best practices, and recognizing the challenges, which may include policy issues, scientific issues, and technological issues." (National Geospatial Advisory Committee, 2011)

Whether the data are online or not, the agreement must define who has what rights to access the data, who has what rights to change or modify the data, and what the methods of data access will be.

Question 64.

Your organization has completed its data inventory and data retention policy has been compiled to overlay the data within the organization's possession.

As outlined in the GDPR, data destruction — designated as the elimination, erasure or clearing of digital content — is classified as a form of data processing. It also means any destruction procedures should follow the specific rules set forth by the regulation. Here are three steps that need to be followed:

Step 1: Step one is obviously to implement the appropriate controls allowing data owners full rights and permissions over their affected content. Companies must provide users with an option to delete all personal data — including sales or browsing histories. It absolutely must be a practical option that stems the flow of new content and eliminates the old as soon as possible.

Step 2: Businesses are also obligated to ensure old data or content is securely erased. Just deleting it via the operating system or server is not enough. In fact, reformatting old drives and magnetic media — including hard drives or audio tapes — is no guarantee, either. Deleted data can often be recovered provided the physical media is available.

Step 3: It's important to properly dispose of?

Answers:

A. Hardware
B. Software
C. Records
D. Cloud storage

The correct answer is A. It's important to properly dispose of the hardware involved, too — not just the digital forms of content. One must employ permanent erasure solutions, such as degaussing, which involves the application of magnetic tape to render devices unreadable or unusable. Physical media may also be shredded, crushed, or incinerated to ensure full compliance.

Question 65.

An organization that suffers a cyber event may be investigated to determine if they had the appropriate policies and procedures in place, along with documented training for their workforce. If the organization had those correct controls in place, this organization is able to prove that they have?

E. Consumer Trust
F. Compliance
G. Accountability
H. Responsibility

The best, correct answer would be C. Accountability. Accountable organizations will be able to show tangible evidence that they have executed both their due care and due diligence as it relates to policy development, implementation, dissemination, training, and follow-up actions ensuring that their workforce is able to apply and comply with those policies and procedures. Consumer trust (Answer A) is a by-product of being accountable, as is Compliance (Answer B). The organization is being responsible (Answer D) by being accountable. Without being accountable, the organization would not have trust. The organization would more than likely not be compliant, nor would they be responsible in protecting their data.

Question 66.

Article 51 of GDPR states that each Member State shall provide for one or more independent public authority to be responsible for monitoring the application of this Regulation, in order to protect the fundamental rights and freedoms of natural persons in relation to processing and to facilitate the free flow of personal data within the Union.

What authority is this?

Answers:

A. Data Protection Officer
B. Member of the EDPB
C. European Data Protection Supervisor
D. Supervisory authority

The correct answer is D. A supervisory authority is defined by the GDPR in GDPR Article 4 (Definitions) as "an independent public authority which is established by a Member State pursuant to Article 51".

Question 67.

Whose core tasks are to supervise the EU institutions to help them be exemplary; public authorities must be beyond reproach when they process personal information.

We do this by monitoring those activities that use (process) personal data or information. The personal data could be yours or that of anyone else who works for or with the EU, including visitors, contractors or beneficiaries of grants.

Answers:

A. Supervisory authority
B. Data protection authority
C. Data protection officer
D. European Data Protection Supervisor

The correct answer is D. The European Data Protection Supervisor (EDPS) is an independent supervisory authority whose primary objective is to ensure that European institutions and bodies respect the right to privacy and data protection when they process personal data and develop new policies.

Question 68.

Under which GDPR article does it articulate that any person who has suffered material or non-material damage as a result of an infringement of this Regulation shall have the right to receive compensation from the controller or processor for the damage suffered.

Answers:

A. Art. 80
B. Art. 77
C. Art. 78
D. Art. 82

The correct answer is D.
Chapter 8 (Art. 77 – 84)Remedies, liability and penalties

Art. 77 Right to lodge a complaint with a supervisory authority
Art. 78 Right to an effective judicial remedy against a supervisory authority
Art. 79 Right to an effective judicial remedy against a controller or processor
Art. 80 Representation of data subjects
Art. 81 Suspension of proceedings
Art. 82 Right to compensation and liability
Art. 83 General conditions for imposing administrative fines

Question 69.

You, a citizen of a Member State, discovers and confirms that your information that is stored with a controller is incorrect. Which GDPR article provides you the right to rectify that discrepancy?

Answers:

A. Art. 16
B. Art. 15
C. Art. 17
D. Art. 19

The correct answer is A.

Chapter 3 (Art. 12 – 23) Rights of the data subject

Art. 12 Transparent information, communication and modalities for the exercise of the rights of the data subject
Art. 13 Information to be provided where personal data are collected from the data subject
Art. 14 Information to be provided where personal data have not been obtained from the data subject
Art. 15 Right of access by the data subject
Art. 16 Right to rectification
Art. 17 Right to erasure ('right to be forgotten')
Art. 18 Right to restriction of processing
Art. 19 Notification obligation regarding rectification or erasure of personal data or restriction of processing

Question 70.

As you assess your prospective processor, what is one topic that is not a priority for you to assess?

Answers:

A. Appropriate technical and organizational measures
B. Processor shall not engage another processor without specific or general written authorization
C. Processing by a processor shall be governed by a contract
D. What data the processor will process

The correct answer is D. What data the processor will process is not part of your assessment of the processor. That is a business decision and may assist you in narrowing your processors with their experience in processing that type of data, however, it would not be a part of your formal assessment of the vendor and their practices.

Question 71.

You are making a purchase on an e-commerce website and a banner at the bottom of the page appears before you can provide your billing and shipping information. This banner articulates what the organization does to protect your information. What is this called?

Answers:

A. Opt-Out
B. Opt-In
C. Privacy Notice
D. Privacy Policy

The correct answer is C. The EU General Data Protection Regulation (GDPR) requires that data controllers provide certain information to people whose information (personal data) they hold and use. A privacy notice is one way of providing this information. This is sometimes referred to as a fair processing notice.

A privacy notice should identify who the data controller is, with contact details for its Data Protection Officer. It should also explain the purposes for which personal data are collected and used, how the data are used and disclosed, how long it is kept, and the controller's legal basis for processing.

Question 72.

Your multinational organization has voluntarily joined and started sharing cybersecurity information with other entities, both public and private within the United States of America. The sharing consists of cyber threat information while protecting classified information, intelligence sources and methods, and privacy and civil liberties.
This sharing of information authorizes companies to monitor and implement defensive measures on their own information systems to counter cyber threats. Second, it provides certain protections to encourage companies voluntarily to share information—specifically, information about "cyber threat indicators" and "defensive measures"—with the federal government, state and local governments, and other companies and private entities. These protections include protections from liability, non-waiver of privilege, and protections from FOIA disclosure, although, importantly, some of these protections apply only when sharing with certain entities.
What Act is this?

Answers:

A. Freedom of Information Act
B. Cybersecurity Information Sharing Act
C. Electronic Communications Privacy Act
D. Federal Trade Commission Act

The correct answer is B. Congress designed CISA to create a voluntary cybersecurity information sharing process that will encourage public and private entities to share cyber threat information while protecting classified information, intelligence sources and methods, and privacy and civil liberties.

Question 73.

You are reviewing your data inventory and determining what characteristics of data have been compiled that create a profile of the data subject. You have reviewed the GDPR, its recitals and definitions of data subjects.
All of the following are definitions of data subjects except?

Answers:

A. Resident of the EU
B. Personal data
C. Citizen of the EU
D. An EU Resident/Citizen located anywhere

The correct answer is B.
Answer A, Resident of the EU, is a data subject of anyone who formally resides within the Union, regardless of citizenship, while that individual is physically within the Union. For example, a non-EU citizen who is studying abroad in the EU.

Answer C, Citizen of the EU, is a data subject who has formal citizenship in the EU while that individual is physically within the Union.

Answer D, an EU Resident/Citizen Located Anywhere, is a data subject for anyone who has residency/citizenship in the EU whose data is being processed, regardless of where the resident/citizen is physically located at the time of processing. For example, a data subject could be an EU citizen, who is located in the US, and who provides personal information during the purchase of a product.

Question 74.

As you and your organization review and assess prospective vendors/processors, you review data sharing implications, adequacy decisions, data subject's rights and appropriate technical and organizational measures.
Which of the following are not privacy matters to consider?

Answers:

A. Geographical location
B. Global Privacy Regulations
C. Cross-border data sharing
D. Competitor's Privacy Strategy

The correct answer is D. Although it would be nice to know what your competitors are doing, it is not a priority for your organization to focus on. The other three answers are and should be taken into consideration.

Question 75.

Data protection and safety is one of the most important things your organization can do if it regularly processes personal data.
Many provisions and stipulations of the GDPR boil down to a simple requirement: ensure the data is safe.
If you manage to do that, you have much less to worry about and all other issues that may arise become a lot easier to solve.
The following are all essential data protection methods except?

Answers:

A. Backups
B. Regulations
C. Pseudonymization
D. Encryption

The correct answer is B. Risk assessment, backups, encryption, pseudonymization, access controls, and destruction are essential to protecting data.

Question 76.

Data subject rights are never absolute. There are conditions and exceptions, but there are also other rights to keep in mind. The right of freedom of expression and information, for instance, can have an impact with regards to the right of erasure.
You're providing an online newsletter. Your client gives their consent to subscribe to the online newsletter that allows you to process all the data on their interests to build a profile of what articles they consult. One year on, they inform you that they no longer wish to receive the online newsletter.
What must your organization do?

Answers:

A. Delete information
B. Remove from newsletter mailing list
C. Request consent again
D. Disclose information collected

The correct answer is A. You must delete all personal data relating to that person collected in the context of the newsletter subscription from your database, including the profile(s) relating to that person.

Question 77.

You are consulting with your information security team on new lifecycle processes.
You are promoting the incorporation of data protection via their technology designs and
infrastructure implementations.
You remember that you can have security without privacy, however, you cannot have privacy
without security.
What design model is this referencing?

Answers:

A. Privacy by Default
B. Privacy by Design
C. Integrity and Confidentiality
D. Privacy Program

The correct answer is B. Privacy by design or data protection by design is when your
organization is developing, designing, selecting and using applications, services and products
that are based on the processing of personal data or process personal data to fulfil their task,
producers of the products, services and applications should be encouraged to take into account
the right to data protection when developing and designing such products, services and
applications and, with due regard to the state of the art, to make sure that controllers and
processors are able to fulfil their data protection obligations.

Answer A, Privacy by Default, is the implementation of appropriate technical and organizational
measures for ensuring that, by default, only personal data which are necessary for each specific
purpose of the processing are processed.

Answer C is one of the six data processing principles.

Question 78.

Your organization is a public authority that processes data and the core activities of the organization consist of processing operations whose scope and purposes require regular and systematic monitoring of data subjects on a large scale.

What does your organization need to designate?

Answers:

A. A Processor
B. A Controller
C. Data Protection Officer
D. A Judicial body

The correct answer is C. Art. 38, Designation of the data protection officer, describes when a DPO is required.

Question 79.

GDPR introduces in Article 5(2) GDPR the principle of accountability. According to this principle, the controller shall be responsible for compliance with the principles listed in Article 5(1) GDPR and addressed above and shall be able to what?

Answers:

A. Demonstrate compliance
B. Implement confidentiality and availability
C. Implement Privacy Notices
D. Implement Privacy Policies

The correct answer is A. You must show evidence that you are compliant with the data protection principles to be viewed as accountable.

Question 80.

You have been in your privacy professional role with your organization for just over one year. You are preparing for your first formal audit of the privacy program. What step of the five-phase audit cycle is this?

Answers:

A. First
B. Second
C. Third
D. Fourth

The correct answer is B. The five-phase audit approach includes: Audit Planning; Audit Preparation; Conducting the Audit; Reporting; and Follow-up.

Question 81.

Which data principle is meaning that it is required to ensure that personal data are accurate and are kept up to date where it is necessary? Personal data that are inaccurate – considering the purposes for their processing – must be deleted or rectified without any delay?

Answers:

A. Proportional
B. Purpose limitation
C. Accuracy
D. Storage limitation

The correct answer is A. Accuracy is the fourth data protection principle.

Question 82.

You have been in your privacy professional role with your organization for just over one year. You have finalized the research, materials and submitted the findings to your organization for their review. What step of the five-phase audit cycle is this?

Answers:

A. First
B. Second
C. Third
D. Fourth

The correct answer is D. The five-phase audit approach includes: Audit Planning; Audit Preparation; Conducting the Audit; Reporting; and Follow-up.

Question 83.

Your organization is finalizing both the privacy policy and the information security policy. They are both drastically different, to include the structure to how they are presented and available for consumption.

They are both presented in with a layered approach. One of them is defining three levels. The top layer is a high-level document containing the controller's policy statement. The next layer is a more detailed document that sets out the security controls that will be implemented to achieve the policy statements. The third layer is the most detailed and contains the operating procedures, which explain how the policy statements will be achieved in practice.

Which policy are we discussing?

Answers:

A. Privacy Policy
B. Information Security Policy
C. Integrity Policy
D. Privacy Notice (layered)

The correct answer is B. The key word is in the second layer description. The security controls that will be implemented.

This question is not trying to trick you. It is to help you focus on key words in the question that are being posed for you to pick up on.

You will have questions that will be vague, however, there will be a key word or term within it that will help you

Question 84.

Ransomware attacks continue to thrive on organizations globally and your organization has determined to become a more resilient organization.
Access controls and verification of identities have become a focal point.
Your information security group has determined to implement a new authentication process that requires more than one verification method. What is this security control called?

Answers:

A. Username and password
B. Tokenization
C. Encryption
D. Multi-factor authentication

The correct answer is D. Multi-factor authentication ensures that a user is who he or she claims to be. The more factors used to determine a person's identity, the greater the trust of authenticity.

Single factor authentication involves the use of simply one of the three available factors solely to carry out the authentication process being requested.

Question 85.

GDPR addresses everything from data collection and sharing to data destruction. As part of respecting the rights of data owners, companies must also provide them with the option to wipe or delete any information in full. This is designated as the "right to be forgotten," or the right to erasure.
After your company has deleted the information, you discover residual magnetism is left behind. What is this called?

Answers:

A. Remanence
B. Deleted file
C. Disposal
D. Residual risk

The correct answer is A. Remanence is the residual magnetism left behind after degaussing or deleting files.

Question 86.

A fair information practices principle, it is the principle stating there should be limits to the collection of personal data, that any such data should be obtained by lawful and fair means and, where appropriate, with the knowledge or consent of the data subject. This is called what?

Answers:

A. Collection limitation
B. Purpose limitation
C. Consent
D. Storage limitation

The correct answer is A. The fair information practice principles are:

(1) The Collection Limitation Principle
(2) The Data Quality Principle
(3) The Purpose Specification Principle
(4) The Use Limitation Principle
(5) The Security Safeguards Principle
(6) The Openness Principle
(7) The Individual Participation Principle
(8) The Accountability Principle

Question 87.

There are four classes of privacy that your organization must understand and control. One of those classes encompasses protection of the means of correspondence, including postal mail, telephone conversations, electronic e-mail and other forms of communicative behavior and apparatus.

Which class is this?

Answers:

A. Information privacy
B. Bodily privacy
C. Territorial privacy
D. Communications privacy

The correct answer is D.

Answer A, Information privacy, is to know when, how and to what extent information about them is communicated to others.

Answer B, Bodily privacy, focuses on a person's physical being and any invasion thereof. Such an invasion can take the form of genetic testing, drug testing or body cavity searches.

Answer C, Territorial privacy, concerns the setting of limits on intrusion into the domestic and other environments such as the workplace or public space. This includes searches, video surveillance and ID checks.

Question 88.

There are four classes of privacy that your organization must understand and control. One of those classes is to know when, how and to what extent information about them is communicated to others.
Which class is this?

Answers:

A. Information privacy
B. Bodily privacy
C. Territorial privacy
D. Communications privacy

The correct answer is A.

Answer B, Bodily privacy, focuses on a person's physical being and any invasion thereof. Such an invasion can take the form of genetic testing, drug testing or body cavity searches.

Answer C, Territorial privacy, concerns the setting of limits on intrusion into the domestic and other environments such as the workplace or public space. This includes searches, video surveillance and ID checks.

Answer D, Communications privacy, encompasses protection of the means of correspondence, including postal mail, telephone conversations, electronic e-mail and other forms of communicative behavior and apparatus.

Question 89.

There are four classes of privacy that your organization must understand and control. One of those classes concerns the setting of limits on intrusion into the domestic and other environments such as the workplace or public space. This includes searches, video surveillance and ID checks.
Which class is this?

Answers:

A. Information privacy
B. Bodily privacy
C. Territorial privacy
D. Communications privacy

The correct answer is C.

Answer A, Information privacy, is to know when, how and to what extent information about them is communicated to others.

Answer B, Bodily privacy, focuses on a person's physical being and any invasion thereof. Such an invasion can take the form of genetic testing, drug testing or body cavity searches.

Answer D, Communications privacy, encompasses protection of the means of correspondence, including postal mail, telephone conversations, electronic e-mail and other forms of communicative behavior and apparatus.

Question 90.

There are four classes of privacy that your organization must understand and control. One of those classes focuses on a person's physical being and any invasion thereof. Such an invasion can take the form of genetic testing, drug testing or body cavity searches.

Which class is this?

Answers:

A. Information privacy
B. Bodily privacy
C. Territorial privacy
D. Communications privacy

The correct answer is B.

Answer A, Information privacy, is to know when, how and to what extent information about them is communicated to others.

Answer C, Territorial privacy, concerns the setting of limits on intrusion into the domestic and other environments such as the workplace or public space. This includes searches, video surveillance and ID checks.

Answer D, Communications privacy, encompasses protection of the means of correspondence, including postal mail, telephone conversations, electronic e-mail and other forms of communicative behavior and apparatus.

Printed in Great Britain
by Amazon